GETTI
RESU
WITHOUT
AUTHORITY

Anne

Very best wishes

Geoff Cox

GETTING
RESULTS
WITHOUT
AUTHORITY

GEOF COX

bookshaker

First Published in Great Britain 2010
by www.BookShaker.com

PRAISE FROM
ROGER HARRISON

Geof Cox has written a concise, readable and complete exposition of a way to acquire greater skill and flexibility to influence others without using formal authority.

This clearly written book presents a simple and practical model for understanding the interpersonal underworld of personal power and influence: a model which in its various incarnations has stood the tests of time and application since its first iteration by David Berlew and myself in the early seventies.

The author goes well beyond those roots, showing ways each of the four styles of influence may be applied to managing conflict, negotiating, working cross-culturally and with remote teams.

The theory comes with a wealth of examples, practice exercises and tips for application, and it will be of interest and utility to anyone who has to get others to get others to do things-which means all of us! I highly recommend it.

Roger Harrison

Roger Harrison is one of the original leaders and practitioners in organisation development. He was also the co-designer with David Berlew of the *Positive Power and Influence Programme*, recognised as one of the first management development programme to address the issue of influence rather than the use of command and control in organisations. His many academic papers can be found in *Collected Papers of Roger Harrison* (McGraw-Hill 1995).

GEOF COX

Geof has over twenty five years of international experience as a management and organisation development consultant, preceded by fifteen years as a line and HR manager in the oil industry with Esso Petroleum. His passions are for designing and facilitating workshops in management and communication skills and facilitating organisation change using large group engagement processes.

He has worked across Europe, Russia, the Middle East, Africa, AsiaPAC and the Americas with managers from most sectors. As a true Brit, Geof works only in English, but is practised in communicating with people where

English is not the native language; so he doesn't just speak louder and slower!

Geof is also a business writer and author. Previous titles include *Ready-Aim-Fire Problem Solving*, *50 Activities for Creativity and Problem Solving* and *25 Role Plays for Interview Training*. He edits a bi-monthly newsletter, *Cuttings*.

Geof loves to find out new ideas and share them with anyone who will listen. He loves to travel to learn about new cultures, and to find more people who will listen! He also likes to retreat to his house on the Isle of Arran in Scotland with his family and dogs.

CONTENTS

Part Two: Developing The Styles

FOREWORD

"One of the conventions of Star Trek is that all alien life forms can communicate with Star Fleet Federation vessels in perfect English. Communication is made via the Universal Translator, a device that permits fluent two-way communication. Sadly no such device exists between employee and managers. All too often communication breaks down between boss and direct report because neither is speaking the same language, albeit they are speaking in a language common to each. The problem lies not in words but in expectation. For example, the boss wants an overview but the employee provides granular detail. Or vice versa. So unlike in Star Trek neither is truly communicating with the other."[1]

This excerpt from a column of mine sets up the themes that Geof Cox addresses in *Getting Results Without Authority*. While Geof's book is not a Universal Translator, it does go a long way to help people to communicate effectively with each other and in so doing, get better results. And while I was specifically thinking about the communication between employees and managers, the same principles are true for anyone you are trying to influence, as Geof points out throughout his insightful book.

First, you need to get on the same wavelength. As anyone in the hospitality business knows, the key to gracious hosting is knowing the preferences of your guests. For example, returnees to a favourite bed and breakfast are likely to have their favourite drinks awaiting them, plus their favourite menu items. Why? Because the owners know what their guests like and do what they can to provide it. The same

---

[1] http://www.fastcompany.com/blog/john-baldoni/grab-n-go-leadership/getting-you-and-your-boss-same-communication-wavelength

goes for people who seek to influence. It is important to know how someone likes to receive information; in short bursts via email or in lengthy reports with plenty of back up material. Oral presentations may be made in short form or long. Knowing the preferred method of the person you are trying to influence is essential to persuasion. So, exchange ideas about how you each like to receive information, how often and about what issues.

Then tune into the conversation. Listen to what the other says. This is not as easy as it sounds because the temptation, often exacerbated by the pressure of deadlines, is to leap to conclusions. The simple answer is to ease up on the schedule and pay attention. Making sure you understand what is being communicated will mean you end up saving a good deal of time.

To increase your influence with senior executives inside organizations, make sure you align your ideas or your project to the corporate objectives. If you know your organization is seeking to grow new markets, then think how your project furthers that aim. Likewise, if your company is stressing quality, look for ways to reduce errors and defects. Influencing an organization is like riding a horse – it is best done facing the direction of travel.

Another key theme of this book is that influence is power but its power does not always depend upon title or rank. People who exert the most influence may not have much power. While most organizations are hierarchical, real influence is often directed laterally as well as upward. Power comes with title but influence stems from trust, chiefly from persuading people that you can do the job. Be prepared. Know your facts as well as you can. This preparation will give you the confidence to present or advocate with energy and enthusiasm. This will lend your case and your team a sense of presence and immediacy.

Getting Results Without Authority is a distillation of Geof's work in helping managers learn better ways of getting things done, on time and on budget, but also with improved clarity and commitment. Teaching is something in which Geof excels and for that reason, this book will be a hands-on guide that will help you become a more effective leader and manager.

If you apply the tips and techniques in his book, you will in effect be creating your own translator. The only problem is that it is not universal. It is specific to each situation. You need to "re-program it" for each relationship you have. But once you do it a few times, you'll become expert and just as in Star Trek be able to communicate with, and influence, any alien (boss, colleague or employee) you encounter!

John Baldoni
Ann Arbor, Michigan, February 2010

John Baldoni is an internationally recognised leadership development consultant, executive coach, author, and speaker. In 2009, Top Leadership Gurus named John one of the world's top 25 leadership experts. John's newest book is *Lead Your Boss: The Subtle Art of Managing Up* (Amacom 2009).

ACKNOWLEDGEMENTS

I am indebted to a great number of people for the content of this book, both for their direct contribution and through their stories and experiences that I have accumulated over the years. I thank them all for the material that they have, often unwittingly, provided.

Roger Harrison first inspired me with his work on power in organisations, organisation culture and common vision leadership while I was still working at Esso in the 1980s. Later, Walt Hopkins and Alison Chamberlain were co-developers of the core model, which I later merged with work done by Pierre Casse at INSEAD Business School.

Chris Argyris, expertly interpreted by Bill Noonan, is the foundation for some of the ideas on the impact of emotion on our behaviour. In this area, I have also been helped through my work with my colleagues and partners in Learning Consortium, whose focus on continuing professional development have helped me to understand and apply the models to myself and my work.

I encountered Peter Block's work early in my career, but did not make the connection with influence and getting results until the early 2000s, when I used his model for stakeholder analysis with a sales team who immediately adopted it for all key account management planning. Since then it has become a firm favourite of participants on my workshops.

I am grateful to the publishers of Pierre Casse (Elsevier Limited) and Peter Block (John Wiley & Sons, Inc.) for their permission to use their material in this book. I am also grateful to Gower Publishing Limited for permission to use the majority of a paper I published on Influence in *The*

Gower Handbook of Management, Fourth Edition, which is the core of chapters 3 and 4. Other sources of inspiration are referenced throughout, with thanks.

Lysiane Bysh and Jem Scanlan, two of the co-presenters of the workshop from which this book is developed, have contributed many ideas over the years and were kind enough to comment on my early drafts of the manuscript. My colleague Frank Penson and my wife Joan also provided very helpful and insightful comments on the content, particularly making sure that my grammar and spelling were consistent throughout. Freda Rollins and David Cleeton-Watkins provided an opportunity for me to implant my ideas into a workshop that they had previously developed, very much my cuckoo hatching in their nest, and Frost & Sullivan have been very active in promoting the workshop during the past 10 years.

My publishers Debbie Jenkins and Joe Gregory of Bookshaker encouraged me to put the ideas in book form, and have provided enormous support and direction through the process.

Finally, I must acknowledge all of the organisations and individuals who have been on the receiving end of my consulting and training in interpersonal skills for the past 25 years. Many of those organisations and individuals contributed the case studies and examples which illustrate the chapters. Names and contexts have been changed to protect both the guilty and the praiseworthy, but their contribution is invaluable.

Geof Cox
New Directions (Communications & Training) Limited
Bristol, England and Isle of Arran, Scotland, February 2010

CHAPTER ONE

INTRODUCTION

"Misunderstandings don't exist -
only the failure to communicate."
ASIAN PROVERB

"A lot of people make the mistake of thinking that getting
results is all there is to the job. Great leaders find a balance
between getting results and how they get them."
ANDY PEARSON

This book is about influence – the process by which one person gets another to do something – which is becoming increasingly important in the new structures and relationships of today's organisations. We would all like more influence. We would all like a greater range of skills to influence people and situations that are crucial to our success. We need to be able to get what we want and need in order to satisfy our own work and personal goals.

As the business environment changes we have to get quicker results and get things done through others. We have to get commitment for projects and deadlines for which we are responsible. We need to get the agreement and cooperation of people who do not work directly for us, but whose outputs are critical to our success. Matrix and project based organisation structures distort working relationships. We often find we do not have the authority to get things done.

But just getting things done is not enough. Today's workforce does not respond positively to anything that is remotely autocratic or authoritarian in style. So even where you do have authority to tell people what to do, you cannot use it without regard to the longer term impact. And in situations where you do not have authority, you cannot afford to upset the other parties, as you will need their continued cooperation on this or future projects. So, you need to develop skills which will not only get what you want, but also build or at least maintain a positive working relationship with the other parties. You need to develop positive influencing skills that have the effect that people do things because they "want to" rather than because they "have to."

The research base for this book covers over 30 years of experience of working with influencing and interpersonal skills in over 35 countries and with people from more than 80 countries. It also builds on the workshop designs and training courses run by myself and a number of partners and consultants, which have culminated in the Getting Results Without Authority course. It is, therefore, a very practical book that will help you to work effectively in today's environment; to be more successful in getting the results you need from your interpersonal relationships. It will give you the tools to analyse work situations to make sure that you do not focus too much on the task objective and put the long term relationship at risk, or spend too much effort on ensuring a good relationship and not achieving the task. It will help you to define when to be flexible and when to be firm. And it will outline the different styles that you can adopt to be able to deal with the different situations and people that you need to influence.

The main theme of this book is to improve interpersonal communications, especially in business. No-one consciously takes on a new project with the intention of sabotaging it, and no-one deliberately sets out to put barriers in their route to success. Yet our presentations don't succeed, our partners get upset and hold grudges against us, and relationships worsen rather than improve when we try to intervene. This book is about understanding why this happens and gives you the skills to get a different result.

The book has been written for people in organisations at any level – anyone who needs to get results in situations where they do not have the positional power of authority – including project managers, project team members, those working in matrix organisations, technical staff, internal consultants, and professional staff. Anyone who does have a position of authority, but does not want to use that authority to tell people what to do, will find the approach used in the book of value.

It is equally applicable to people who want to influence action in the community or in social environments, and, although not expressly included in the examples and content, it does of course apply to personal relationships. It is a practical tool to help people in all walks of life to become more successful in influencing others, getting their message across, building relationships and achieving their goals.

Each chapter contains a number of simple practice exercises to help develop underused or undervalued skills, and to assist observation and understanding of the environment in which you operate. As well as the development exercises, there are examples and case studies taken from real life situations throughout the book which will help you to transfer the learning to your situation.

The book is divided into three parts:

INTRODUCTION

Part 1 – The Influence Arena analyses the working environment of the early 21st century and the growing need for the use of positive influence skills.

- The first two chapters set the scene, analysing the current working environment and the impact this has on the way we need to interact with each other. They look at the particular problems that are caused by matrix and project structures and how we need to develop our personal sources of power.
- Chapter 4 introduces a four style model for analysing effective influence behaviour, the impact of each style, and how to recognise the styles in yourself and others. A self-analysis questionnaire is included to help determine your own preferences and their implications.
- Chapter 5 takes a look behind the scenes at what is going on in our heads, often sub-consciously. Our emotions and feelings have a massive impact on the effectiveness of our communication, and this chapter goes some way to helping you understand how and why, as well as giving some practical tips in how to deal with situations where we get triggered into an unhelpful response.

Part 2 – Developing the styles is a series of four chapters on the influence styles that you need to be successful in that working environment.

- Chapter 6 introduces Part 2 with some navigation tips to the chapters that follow which provide in depth knowledge of the four styles, with each having some more development exercises to help improve both your skill and your comfort with using each style.
- Chapter 7 looks at how you can make effective deals by balancing demands and exchanges. Chapter 8 investigates the use of rational arguments to find

solutions. Chapter 9 focuses on the skill of listening empathetically to generate understanding. Chapter 10 shows how you can build cooperation through sharing inspiring visions of the future.

Part 3 – Application introduces some tools and approaches to deal effectively with real life situations.

- Chapter 11 introduces a planning guide and a 5-Step approach to analysing situations to help you make an informed choice about the most successful approach to critical influence situations. Chapter 12 looks at how you can get positive outcomes in the more difficult situations where there is either greater complexity or deeper conflicts of interest or differences of opinion which need to be resolved.

- The last chapter focuses on further development, with suggestions for training courses and other resources to deepen understanding and skills in interpersonal communication. Finally, there is a glossary of terms used in an Appendix for those readers who are not familiar with some of the management theories and concepts referred to in the book.

A final word and reminder on the focus of this book – it is about establishing positive, long term working relationships at the same time as achieving short term task goals. Influence is used in a positive frame and not with the negative connotation that the term has in some other languages, where it is associated with manipulation. Most of the skills and behaviours outlined in the book can be used to manipulate people and trick them into doing what you want. This may be effective in the short term but is not sustainable in the long term, as any observer of the political system will know. Throughout the book, I am assuming that people will be using the skills with integrity, and with a positive intent.

INTRODUCTION

PART ONE

THE INFLUENCE ARENA

CHAPTER TWO

THE INFLUENCE ARENA

*"Leadership is about the ability to influence people by
personal attributes and behaviours."*
JOHN ADAIR

*"In organisations, real power and energy is generated
through relationships. The patterns of relationships and the
capacities to form them are more important than tasks,
functions, roles, and positions."*
MARGARET WHEATLEY

The influence arena, the environment in which we operate
in our professional and personal lives, is getting more
complex by the day. Organisation structures and cultures
are notoriously slow to adapt, but in the face of the
information and communication revolution of the last 20
years, the reality if not the formal structure of relationships
at work has seen a radical change. You cannot tell someone
what to do anymore and expect them to do it. Command
and control and hierarchy are not respected. Where it still
exists, it is not effective and generally leads to high staff
turnover as people leave to find a better environment, or
lands the protagonists in court on charges of bullying. Staff
are demanding a different way of being managed or led.

Where structures have adapted to meet the current
challenges, we have seen the emergence of matrix and project
based organisations. These structures demand a different

approach to getting things done – the structure here prohibits the manager or leader from telling others what to do.

Both changes demand influence – the process by which one person gets another to do something. This chapter looks at the issues of working in modern organisations and the growing need for positive influence skills to get people to do what we want, so that the other party does it because they "want to" rather than because they "have to".

THE MODERN ORGANISATION

Increasingly we need to get people who do not work directly for us to do things that are central to the success of our own job. They are often working to different priorities and have a different goal. They don't see the urgency and the need the way we do. Some organisational changes are pushing this development at a faster and faster rate:

- The rate of pace of change is continuing to increase, meaning that most organisations find themselves in a constant state of flux. Any semblance of stability drawn on an organisation chart is likely to be out of date by the time someone has drawn it. The reality is that the reporting structures and roles will have changed, and the people who deliver the results will be different.

- There has been a massive growth in the use of project teams to help drive the changes necessary to make the organisation adapt and be successful. A project team will bring people from several different departments, and often different organisations, together to complete a specific goal. The project manager is coordinating the overall drive towards the goal, but does not have any line authority over the team members.

- Many of the non-core activities of organisations are outsourced, which means that we need people working in other independent organisations to do things for us. Increasingly, these outsourced operations are moving offshore into other countries where the labour pool may be cheaper or more plentiful.

- Organisation structures are getting flatter and flatter with each reorganisation. Management levels are being trimmed and spans of control are increased. It is becoming impossible for managers to have detailed knowledge of what everyone is doing in their teams, which is a pre-requisite for command and control. It is also more difficult to identify hierarchical authority patterns and responsibilities.

- Work is being re-distributed according to the appropriate person rather than a job function, for example: responsibility for quality control and checking is now the responsibility of the line operator, not the quality control department. In many organisations, delegation of responsibilities to the lowest possible level means that more people are interacting to make decisions that used to be in the hands of the all-powerful line manager or supervisor.

- Position in the hierarchy, or seniority is becoming less important than ability in the choice of the right person for the job. So empowered workers from very junior positions can take the lead on major projects and take operational decisions in the organisation.

- The demographic shift from Baby Boomers to Generation X and Generation Y[2] in the workplace has brought a change in attitude towards authority.

---

[2] For explanations of the Baby Boomer and X and Y Generations, see the Glossary of terms in Appendix 1

People are marching to a different drummer and will not respond to being told. They are demanding more say, more responsibility and more control over their own destiny. They want to believe in what they are doing and make a contribution, not just pick up their pay cheque.

- The recognition of the success of participative processes and empowerment further reduces the opportunity to use the traditional tell style. Someone who feels that they have more control and influence over their own work, is more likely to take an interest and improve their performance. Those who design the organisations of today recognise this and build processes that integrate efforts towards a common goal, thus reducing the need for being given direction.

All of these changes are causing a fundamental shift in the way things are achieved in organisations. No longer does your position in the hierarchy determine what gets done, as the responsibility for action is in the hands of the project leader or the empowered individual pursuing their own clear goals and objectives. People need to be influenced to do things, not be told. The skill of influence has to exist right across the organisation, and at all levels. Everyone needs to influence others in order to complete their own jobs. Never before has the skill of influencing been more important for the future success of organisations of all sizes and functions, and for those who work in them.

JAZZ – THE NEW METAPHOR

Warren Bennis, the pioneer of the field of leadership studies once said: *"I used to think that running an organisation was equivalent to conducting a symphony orchestra. But I don't think that's quite it; it's more like jazz. There is more improvisation."*

The metaphor of the symphony orchestra is the equivalent of the traditional organisation – groups of specialists contributing to a total goal that the conductor is directing. The sections of the orchestra are the equivalent of the departments of an organisation. The leader of each section is responsible for the specialists in his group, just like the departmental manager. They operate independently of the other sections, producing their specialist part of the output. The conductor is the person with the overall authority to pull the individual parts together to create the symphony. The orchestra cannot do it on its own as there is not the ability to communicate across the stage or hear what other sections are doing. Equally, they are unable to switch jobs across the sections and understand the symphony from a different perspective. They are reliant on someone else making sense of the whole, while they focus on their own specialism.

From his experience of working in a symphony orchestra as well as being one of the world's leading jazz vibraphonists, Gary Burton makes the observation *"There is often a battle between the conductor and the members, with the members playing up and playing games to try to upset the conductor."* In the same article for Fast Company magazine[3], he relates an experience of one of his classical friends when she was appearing as a violin soloist with the New York Philharmonic. *"At rehearsal Zubin Mehta was conducting and the players were being incredibly disrespectful. They weren't paying attention, they were talking to each other, listening to the ballgame on the radio. She turned to one of her friends in the orchestra and said, 'I had no idea things were this bad.' He replied, 'We're all on good behaviour tonight because you're here.'"* Burton's conclusion: *"The conductor has all of the control, the players are disempowered, so they abdicate.*

---

[3] Lessons on business from a jazz legend. The Gary Burton Trio, by Michael Schrage, Fast Company, Issue 06, Dec 1996/Jan 1997, Page 110.

Exactly what goes on in corporate organisations – the orchestra conductor metaphor is not helpful."

So what is jazz leadership?

Max De Pree in his book Leadership Jazz[4] explains it thus: *"One way to think about leadership is to consider a jazz band. Jazz-band leaders must choose the music, find the right musicians, and perform – in public. But the effect of the performance depends on so many things – the environment, the volunteers playing in the band, the need for everyone to perform as individuals and as a group, the absolute dependence of the leader on the members of the band and the need of the leader for the followers to play well. A jazz band is an expression of servant leadership. The leader of a jazz band has the beautiful opportunity to draw the best out of the other musicians. We have much to learn from jazz-band leaders, for jazz, like leadership, combines the unpredictability of the future with the gifts of individuals."*

Frank Barrett, Professor of Organisation Behaviour at the US Naval Postgraduate School (and a jazz pianist) says: *"When the players get together they do what managers find themselves doing: fabricating and inventing novel responses without a pre-scripted plan and without certainty of outcomes; discovering the future that their action creates as it unfolds[5]."*

That is not to say that a jazz combo is a democratic or laissez-faire organisation compared to the autocratic orchestra. As Gary Burton points out, *"There is always a strong leader in a jazz group – the difference is that the jazz leader wants strong players who can challenge each other, not yes-men/women – but the vision is always mine."*

---

[4] Leadership Jazz: The Essential Elements of a Great Leader, Max De Pree, Dell Publishing,1993.
[5] Creativity and Improvisation in Jazz and Organizations: Implications for Organizational Learning, Frank J. Barrett, Organization Science Vol.. 9, No.5, September-October 1998.

For organisations who have prided themselves on minimal risk-taking, the new world of fast cycle change is daunting. No longer do they have the luxury of long lead times, opportunities to pilot or engineer-out problems (or have lengthy rehearsals). They need to operate more in the here-and-now, creating and implementing simultaneously with the inherent risk taking, like a jazz band.

Leadership in the jazz world is all about personal qualities not scientific methodology. It is about challenging, continually listening, encouraging high performance from others, building the future that fits in partnership with all the stakeholders, playing a support role when you are not soloing – and encouraging everyone to take the lead. Getting results in this environment is all about influence, not control.

The creation of Miles Davis's most famous and influential album *Kind of Blue* is an example of what is possible in jazz leadership. Celebrating its 51st birthday in 2010, it is the most commercially successful jazz recording of all time and still sells in large numbers. From a leadership perspective, Davis took some massive risks – he brought together some of the great names in jazz of the time, sat them in a recording studio with no music or rehearsal time, and just encouraged everyone to work together, build on each other's ideas and listen intently to what was being played. His risk taking was rewarded, *Kind of Blue* was recorded in two sessions totalling only eight hours, and most were first takes, despite the fact that the band members had never played together before that day. The spontaneity, lack of preconceived ideas and freshness that Davis created, so mirrors what organisations are trying to create in their leadership style that it has become a Harvard University case study in leadership.[6]

---

[6] Kind of Blue: Pushing Boundaries with Miles Davis, Prof. Robert D. Austin and Carl Størmer, reported in HBS Working Knowledge, April 2009.

WORKING IN PROJECT & MATRIX ORGANISATIONS[7]

What is meant by matrix management? Wikipedia defines it as "a type of organisational management in which people with similar skills are pooled for work assignments.[8]" It is often depicted as in Figure 2-1, where the organisation is managed through two lines of command – one line based on the functions of Research, Production, Sales, Finance, and the other line based on Product lines A, B and C. So someone working on Product A in Sales will have a dual reporting relationship to a Sales Manager responsible for overall sales and to the Product Manager who has the overall responsibility for the product.

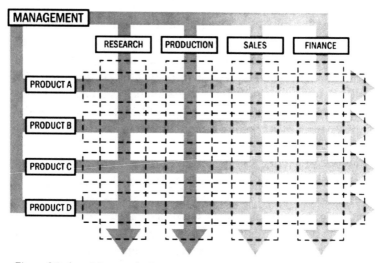

Figure 2-1: A matrix organisation

---

[7] Definitions of terms used can be found in the Glossary at Appendix 1.

[8] http://en.wikipedia.org/wiki/Matrix_management

A matrix might also be drawn with respect to geography and function, or projects and functions, or even three-dimensionally product / function / geography. The matrix may be stronger in one dimension than the other, usually depicted by having "dotted line" relationships versus "straight line" relationships; the straight line usually taking precedence, or they may be balanced where there is no priority. How they are drawn is usually a reflection of the priorities and tensions that exist in the environment in which the organisation operates. A typical matrix in an engineering company is drawn between function and project reflecting the tensions between maintaining the standards and expertise in engineering and the need to deliver projects. In a product driven, international company like an FMCG company, a three way matrix might be drawn between geography, product and function reflecting the tensions between the demands of the local marketplace, the product range, and the cross-functional working to deliver the product to market.

Many people who are in such an organisation structure will be only too well aware of some of the frustrations of working in a matrix:

- *"It's impossible to get any work done around here. There is always someone who has an interest even in the smallest of decisions."*
- *"I don't know what they do or how to get them involved."*
- *"I have one boss who says I should focus on 'X' and another who says focus on 'Y'."*
- *"No-one knows who is responsible anymore."*
- *"How do I get things done when all of my team reports to a different manager?"*
- *"I have the responsibility for the project completion but I don't control any of the resources."*

- *"How do I know if something is being done right when the person doing the job is in a different country and doesn't even work for our company?"*
- *"The project team is located on 3 different continents and time zones, so that we are seldom all in our offices at the same time. Yet efficient communication is the key to our success. How do you make that work?"*

Given the difficulties that are typically voiced, it is hard to accept that a matrix organisation is worth retaining. In fact, after being widely embraced in the 1970s and 1980s, matrix structures did decline in popularity and more hierarchical structures returned for their ease of communication and simplicity. But the matrix is now back, along with its sister structure, the project based organisation. It is back as it reflects the complexity of the business environment which demands that organisations innovate faster and leverage their resources more effectively. The matrix, if well structured and managed, improves the quality and speed of business decisions. It does this by focusing cross-functional expertise in responsive, customer facing groupings that reflect the fluid and complex environment in which the organisation operates.

It is the dual (and multiple) reporting relationship that most often leads to the frustrations and confusions voiced by those caught up in the matrix net. Their cry is for the simplicity and clarity of the hierarchy, which would not reflect the reality of the environment. The frustrations felt are even greater where people have not been adequately trained in working in the matrix, or if the matrix has been implemented badly. If those managing do not understand how to get results in the structure, there is little hope for the rank and file workers. Too often managers waste their energy in a fight for control in a structure where no overall control is a deliberate design feature:

CASE STUDY: THE VICE-PRESIDENT BATTLEGROUND

When I was consulting to a company in the 1990s in Switzerland, they were trying to implement a matrix structure under orders from their US parent. It took the senior executives nearly 18 months to stop fighting amongst themselves for ultimate control and find a way of getting the structure to work. The conversation in the Board meetings was *"I am Executive Vice-President for Marketing, so I am in control of Marketing in Russia"* vs. *"I am Executive Vice-President for Russia, so I am in control of Marketing in Russia"*. Only after some considerable effort did the two protagonists eventually see the way forward and say: *"How do we work together to deliver a marketing operation in Russia that delivers the best value to the Company."* In the meantime a lot of blood was shed while this and similar conversations took place across the whole organisation. The staff were left confused and frustrated while their managers conducted personal battles and left the strategy and operational plans in tatters.

People working in a matrix have to recognise that confusion and conflict is inherent. If there is too much clarity, then there is no need for a matrix. A matrix will have complexity, multiple objectives and divided loyalties. It forces communication between the matrix partners to align goals and ensure role clarity. This is the strength of the matrix. The corollary is that to work effectively in a matrix structure requires highly developed skills in listening, agreement building, collaboration, negotiation, strategic thinking, and self awareness. Matrix working requires that you understand your impact on others and have skills in communicating effectively with people from different functions and cultures, often across large distances which require less face-to-face contact. These skills are not naturally present in simple hierarchies, and therefore trying to impose a matrix or project structure on a traditional hierarchy, without some organisation and management development work is doomed to failure.

As there is little authority, you have to find as many ways as possible to get results without authority.

THE INFLUENCE ARENA

So, the influence arena is complex and getting more complex by the day.

Matrix and project organisation structures have re-emerged as the structures of choice reflecting the reality of the complex and rapidly changing business environment. Organisations are getting better results by capitalising on the benefits of the matrix and mitigating the downsides. But there is still a need to develop the personal communication skills that are needed to make the structures work.

Demographic changes and the growth of the confident, free-agent Generations X and Y in the workplace have further added to the demise of the "tell and sell" approach to organisation and management communication. The new workers demand more participation, more responsibility, have little respect for authority and want more control over their own lives – and if they don't get it, they are confident enough to leave and move on to another organisation.

The metaphor of the leader as a symphony orchestra conductor is being replaced by the leadership style of the jazz combo. Leaders are expected to play a support role as well as a lead role, empowering their team members. The pace of change requires improvisation and real time innovation, risk taking and flexibility.

The influence arena for managers and leaders is changing. All of these issues of working in modern organisations demonstrate that in order to get results, you cannot rely on authority, even if you have it. You have to rely on your personal ability to influence people to do what you want, to find the common interest and encourage cooperation.

DEVELOPMENT EXERCISES

ORGANISATION STRUCTURES AND STYLES OF MANAGEMENT

- Look carefully at the organisations you know. What similarities and differences do you see? How well do they reflect the environment in which they operate? Does the hierarchy or matrix work well? What could be improved?

- Think of the managers and leaders you know. How does their style reflect the structure in which they operate? Is their style complementary or contradictory? In what ways is their approach effective? Why? In what ways is their approach ineffective? Why?

- What structures do you operate in at work and in other situations (community, social, voluntary)? How do the leaders get things done? How effective are they? What styles and approaches seem to work best, in your view?

THE INFLUENCE ARENA

CHAPTER THREE

CAPITALISING ON PERSONAL SOURCES OF POWER & AUTHORITY[9]

"Over the years, leaders consistently have chosen power rather than productivity. They would rather be in control than have the organization work at optimal efficiency. And now there's another belief surfacing: When risk runs high, power must be wielded by only a few people. Just the opposite is true. Reflective leaders, including those in the military, have learned that the higher the risk, the more we need everyone's commitment and intelligence."

MARGARET WHEATLEY

"What truly matters in our lives is measured through conversation. Our dialogue with customers, employees, peers, and our hearts is the most powerful source about where we stand."

PETER BLOCK

The last chapter identified a major issue created by the working environment in the 21st Century – you do not have the direct authority or resources to complete your work goals without getting someone else to do something

---

[9] Parts of this chapter were first published as *Influencing* by Geof Cox in *The Gower Handbook of Management, Fourth Edition*, D. Lock, ed., Gower, Aldershot, 1998. Reproduced with permission from Gower.

for you. To make sure you do this in a positive way, you need to tap into (and build) your sources of power in order to influence others – and you need to make sure that the power you use (and are seen to use) has a positive impact on the other parties we interact with, so that you achieve your twin objectives of getting what you want whilst building or maintaining a positive relationship.

This chapter investigates where your power comes from, how to build your positive sources of power and how you can pro-actively build trust and credibility with those with whom you need to interact.

POWER AND INFLUENCE

If influence is the process by which someone gets another person to do something, power is the resource that the person uses in order to influence. An act of influence of one person on another means that the influencer has used one or more sources of power to encourage the other party to change their behaviour or to do something. What sources of power do we have and use?

One source of legitimate power is position power. This is the power that derives from the position that the person holds in the hierarchy of control and authority in an organisation. But not all of us are managers and have this power source.

Other sources of power include:

- Coercive power
- Resource power
- Information power
- Association power
- Expert power
- Personal power

Coercive power is the power of superior force. It is based on fear. The existence of the physical power, or at least the belief in the other party that you possess the power, is often enough to influence (which is why it is so important that the impact of power sources is carefully considered). In organisations, and in society in general, coercive power is the least respected, and the one that has the most negative connotations – threatening, bullying, violence, detaining by force, and dictating.

CASE STUDY: THE BULLYING MANAGER

Jane was the director of a regional office. She had an autonomous role in running the local operation without interference from headquarters, so long as targets and standards were met. She ruled by fear. Staff turnover was high, either because people left or she fired them for disagreeing with her or being in any way critical of the way the office was run. If a target was not achieved, it was the fault of the manager or staff member concerned, and Jane would routinely berate them in front of everyone in the office. Any idea for improvement was taken as a personal attack on her own ability. Her staff meetings were opportunities for her to tell staff where they were going wrong. When she asked someone to complete a task, she gave little or no explanation about what she wanted. The only way you found out was required was when you presented the result to have it thrown out – it was nothing like what she wanted. Jane would then mutter loudly to everyone in earshot that the only way to get anything done properly was to do it herself. People were incompetent, and she would disappear into her office like a martyr to work late on re-doing everything. The atmosphere was so toxic that staff were most worried when Jane was pleasant and friendly – they didn't believe it and were afraid about what was coming next.

Resource power, sometimes referred to as *reward power*, is the use of valued resources as a basis for influencing others. Thus a manager may use the ability to control a pay increase or allocate interesting work to influence a staff member. A matrix colleague may control the resources needed for a project to succeed. In essence, using resource power to influence is exchanging what you want done for something the other party desires.

The use of resource power is often felt negatively through the actual or perceived restriction or removal of resources. Its impact can also be interpreted as manipulation or bribery if the deal is seen to be unbalanced.

CASE STUDY: AN EMPOWERING MANAGER

Pierre ran a product development department. Each member of his team was given an individual product to focus on, with clear targets for development costs and timeframes. What was most appreciated by his team was the way that Pierre delegated total control of the budget for the project and negotiated the necessary engineer and technician time needed with all of the other managers involved. When Pierre gave you a project, he delegated total responsibility along with all of the resources necessary. By way of reward for successful completion, Pierre would promise, and deliver, future work that was directly connected with the interests and strengths of each individual. His product development department was known throughout the company as a place where people as well as products were developed.

Information power is the power to restrict (negative) or allow (positive) access to information which others need. It is therefore similar in its application to resource power, and is often associated with the position power of manager or boss. However, in modern organisation structures and with the growth of information and communication technology, important sources of information are now located at all levels and positions, so information power can therefore be claimed and used effectively by a large number of people.

CASE STUDY: THE DATABASE MANAGER

Sandy was responsible for managing the database in a small charity. He had all of the financial and operating information at his fingertips, though, because the IT system was not particularly sophisticated, it was not readily accessible to the project managers in the organisation. Sandy used this power to his advantage. He knew that when managers needed operational statistics each month in order to compile the reports to their funders, they would need to come to him and ask for the information. He knew the information they needed every month and could easily set up a system with his team to provide it pro-actively. He could even allow the project managers to link directly with the team member who was dealing with that data. He could modify the systems so that they were more transparent. But Sandy deliberately kept the system complex and user unfriendly. He did not inform his team of the data links that existed, preferring to keep them occupied in unconnected tasks. This left him as the only person who knew how to navigate the database in order to manipulate the data from the different areas that created the information that managers required. He had no apparent gain from this approach, except the personal enjoyment of seeing all of his colleagues having to come to him and plead their case month after month.

Association power is the access to influential people and networks both inside and outside the organisation. Often people need access to such networks or individuals to facilitate their own work, and so the connections they have is a source of power. Like information power, association power used to be the domain of the manager or someone with position power, but now many more people act as gatekeepers and have wide networks and therefore have access to this power.

CASE STUDY: A HIGHER STATUS FRIEND

Alice ran a number of projects in a large multinational oil company. She had been in the role for five years, and had built a formidable network, mainly through the projects that she worked on. These included people in affiliate organisations around the world, as well as suppliers, customers and a vast range of different people in her home country. But even with this wide network, she often came across a situation where she did not know the right person to contact for a specific piece of information. On one occasion, she was working on a small, but important PR project and needed access to some highly confidential information on oil field reserves in order to ensure accuracy of a press release. She knew no-one in the small, tight-knit team who did the field forecasting work. But she knew the Director of Exploration and Production through some work she had done on a safety case on one of the offshore platforms during the previous year. The field asset team reported to this Director. One phone call to the Director and the required access was provided to the head of the asset team (with the authority of the Director to disclose the information needed). She had the data she required.

Expert power is the power that comes from someone's skill, knowledge or expertise. As it derives from the respect and acknowledgement of the power by the other party, it is felt as one of the most positive sources of power. A specialist department or consultant, acknowledged as an expert in their field, will find that their recommendations and suggestions are readily accepted. Expert power is granted by the receiver, not claimed by the influencer. As the influencer you can claim to be an expert, but if the other party does not recognise and accept this, you have no expert power. And if you claim it and it is found that you do not have the expertise, then you seriously undermine your credibility and your ability to influence in the future.

CASE STUDY: THE APPLICATION SPECIALIST

Tariq knew his way around all of the software being used in the warehouse. He was only a basic level operator, but had a recognised knack of being able to fix any problem, find a workaround to any system error, or help anyone in the warehouse to understand what they needed to do. He had no extra training, and had no formal position, but everyone from warehouse manager to fork-lift driver would go directly to Tariq the minute they had a problem. It was quicker than calling the Help Desk or trying to search the FAQs on the application. They also got an answer that worked, and one that they could understand. Eventually, the Help Desk staff started to call Tariq themselves when they received a call that they could not answer easily, and he was co-opted onto the application design team whenever a modification or update was planned. Tariq had no interest in moving into IT, even though a job was offered, he enjoyed working in the warehouse and helping people whenever he could. To everyone there, he was a powerful expert.

Personal power is the power you have through your own personal characteristics, charisma, and the trust and respect others have for you. As the name implies, this power resides in the person, not in the position or role that the person carries out, and for this reason it is highly regarded and sought after. Like expert power it is given by the consent of those over whom it is exercised, and is therefore highly effective but fragile, needing continual nurturing and renewal.

CASE STUDY: THE POWER QUIZ

This quiz has been around the internet a number of times – I first saw it in 1999. It makes the point about the impact of personal power on all of us:

- Name the ten wealthiest people in the world.
- Name the last ten Wimbledon champions.
- Name the last ten winners of best male or female vocalist award.
- Name eight people who have won the Nobel or Pulitzer prize.
- The last ten Academy Award winners for best picture?
- The last five World Champions in any sport?

How did you do? With the exception of trivia hounds, none of us remember the headliners of yesterday too well. It is surprising how quickly we forget. And these are the best in their fields.

Here's another quiz. See how you do on this one:

- Name ten people you enjoy spending time with.
- Name ten people who have taught you something worthwhile.
- Name five friends who have helped you in a difficult time.
- List eight teachers/mentors who have aided your journey through life.
- Name half-a-dozen heroes whose stories have inspired you.

Easier?

Position power, as already defined, is the power that derives from the position that the person holds in the hierarchy of control and authority in an organisation. It can be seen as a combination of some of the other sources of power, as well as being an independent source of power. It is essentially a combination of coercive, resource, association and information power in various mixes depending on the person and the circumstances, and therefore is likely to be viewed in a negative – albeit legitimate – light.

CASE STUDY: LESSONS FROM A PRINCIPLED LEADER[10]

This is the story of Fred Burton, principal of Wickliffe Elementary School in Arlington, Ohio. Many in the school system would recognise Burton's description of his typical workday as "a little like holding hands with a tornado."

The school is home to the Ohio teacher of the year and music teacher of the year in 2002. It has been recognised as an Ohio BEST school, and National Public Radio spent an entire day on site, interviewing students and staff for an expanded feature on progressive education.

On a typical day, children head straight for the door to the playground, Burton stands in the middle of the hallway, watching, listening, saying hello and smiling warmly to all who pass him. He notices a small child picking up a student picture that has fallen off the wall in the rush and carefully places it back in position. And a few days later, at the weekly school "town meeting," he tells all the students about the first grader who took time to save someone's precious piece of art. He asks the boy to stand up, and he

---

[10] This story was first published by Tom Terez on his website www.betterworkplacenow.com, from where copies of the full article and many others which demonstrate the use of personal power can be found. The abridged version is printed here with permission.

does so, surprised but smiling. The school responds with a big round of applause.

Being present

Burton's leadership style can be summed up in two words: being present. No matter how hectic things get, he makes a point of reaching out to absorb all that's happening. He routinely leaves his office to spend time with students and teachers. He's constantly looking for positive stories (like the one about the artwork rescuer), and he makes a point of telling them again and again. He devoutly follows what he calls the 95% Rule: Spend 95% of your time trying to understand people and 5% making judgements.

The power of positive questions

When a parent is concerned about their child, the resulting investigation and strategy is not a confrontational inquest, instead Burton listens, asks questions, listens some more. He becomes a coach, getting the teachers to visualise a meeting with the parents with a positive outcome and rehearsing the meeting.

Efficiency vs. effectiveness

"Organisations are not machines with precision parts," Burton says. *"They involve people and relationships."* When we hurry our conversations or avoid conversations altogether, people feel dismissed - and might be back with bigger issues and deeper problems. We pay for our speed later on.

Technology doesn't help. While it's tempting to dash off several quick e-mail messages instead of calling or meeting someone, e-mail gives the sender no opportunity to read non-verbal cues, pose questions, engage in conversation, or make discoveries. *"Technology as a whole has increased speed,"* Burton says. *"And speed is the enemy of quality."* He recalls a visit from a Russian education administrator who seemed stunned by all the beepers, laptops, and cell phones. *"You're too accessible,"* the visitor said, shaking his head. *"You can never focus on things that matter."*

The effect of being present
Burton tells the story of an art class asked to draw a tree. The children go about their work with impressive efficiency. Within 10 minutes, everyone has a tree. But after the teacher leads them outside, and they take another, closer look at the bark and branches, the smell of wood and leaves - they look at trees - really look ... for the first time. When they return to class, their creations are entirely different. The drawn and crafted branches leap from the pages. What makes the difference? Burton says *"They took their time. By intentionally looking, they created artwork that was very rich."*

This is an example of someone with a lot of position power, preferring instead to utilise their personal power.

POSITION POWER VERSUS PERSONAL POWER

When looking at power in organisations, it is easy just to differentiate between position and personal power, where position power incorporates the use of other associated sources, and personal power includes the use of expert and association power. Getting results without authority requires you to maximise your personal power sources, as position power is not available, or inappropriate. Those who do have position power will also prefer to get results through the use of personal power rather than suffer the potentially negative interpretation of position power. We would all prefer that people did things for us because they "want to" rather than because they "have to."

Although formal organisations have moved on, many traditional behaviours continue, and managers continue to de-motivate employees by resorting to the KITA or Kick In The Ass (mainly figuratively speaking) that Frederick

Herzberg[11] identified, which achieves a result but needs frequent repetition. The more the kicks, the less the quality of the relationship.

The days of "putting up" with poor management are fast declining. In the new forms of organisation, managers need to influence outside of their line of authority in order to achieve their task goals, and cannot therefore afford to endanger their relationships with others. The other party may not work directly for them, so will be able to say no with far less fear of the consequences than a direct subordinate. The manager will also need to influence the same person again in the future, so they cannot afford the relationship to be compromised.

The generations that are now becoming the majority in the workplace, Generations X and Y, are also less likely to accept authoritarian rule. They expect and demand more involvement in decision making, and have confidence in their employability – independent of the organisation that currently employs them. They have been dubbed the "free agent" and "confident" generation, happy to work hard and stay loyal as long as their needs are met, and leave if they are not. And, as Marcus Buckingham and Curt Coffman put it so well in their landmark book *First Break All The Rules*[12]: "people leave managers, not organisations."

However, one of the problems with position power is that you cannot deny or give it up. Even if you do not use it, you still have it. If you are in a management role, or in a more senior perceived position to those you are trying to influence,

[11] *One more time: how do you motivate employees?*, Herzberg, F., Harvard Business Review, vol. 46 no 1, Jan/Feb 1968, pp53-62.

[12] First, Break All the Rules: What the World's Greatest Managers Do Differently, Buckingham, M and Coffman, C, Simon & Schuster; 1999.

then you have position power, whether you like it or not. And the impact of not recognising this can be devastating.

CASE STUDY: GOOD INTENTIONS BACKFIRE

A director of a multi-national company had all of the best intentions in mind when he visited a location in the early hours of the morning to greet the workers on the shop floor at the start of the shift. He wanted to introduce himself as the new director and build some direct, personal relationships with the workforce.

He deliberately chose the start of the shift not a "normal" director's visit during the 9-5 day so he could meet the workers on their terms. He wanted to show that he was approachable and willing to engage.

The impact of his visit had the opposite effect – there was an immediate walk-out. The director's intended, non-threatening and interested questions such as *"Hello, what are you doing?"* were heard as threatening, checking, controlling and authoritarian.

A salutary lesson in the difference between intent and impact in the use of power. You may **intend** not to use position power (you are interested in them as individuals) but the **impact** on the receiver will be different due to the position relationship (you are checking up and micro-managing me).

Some of the signs of position power are varied – and sometimes not totally transparent to the user. Using authority and applying rewards and sanctions associated with your position are clear uses of position power, whereas asking someone to come to your office or getting them to call you are less obvious signs. Using rules, policies and procedures are also uses of positional power. They are associated with your role, even if you are not the author of the rule or policy. Other signs may be more in perception than reality. For instance, most employees who are experiencing organisation change will assume that other, more senior people have information that they are withholding (often correctly!) which would be seen as a negative use of position power.

Personal power is more positive in its application, so even if you have position power, you may want to use your personal power sources more than your position power sources to get a better impact when seeking results. Personal power is, however, not as tangible as position power. You have to work very hard to build it and maintain it, yet it is often built from a myriad of small, behavioural actions. You don't create your personality and charisma in one act. It is a combination of many individual and often minor interactions with others.

The more you do things for other people and acknowledge them, the more they will do for you. Robert Cialdini[13] recognises this as one of the fundamental principles of the psychology of influence – *reciprocation* – the simple give and take idea. And Steven Covey[14] uses the idea of the "emotional bank balance" to describe how you build positive relationships with others – whenever you acknowledge or do something positive for someone, they make a credit deposit in their emotional bank balance with respect to you, from which you may then make withdrawals. So you have to give to get, and you cannot go into overdraft!

You can enhance your personal power by developing and demonstrating your:

---

[13] *Influence: The Psychology of Persuasion,* Cialdini, Robert B, HarperCollins, 1984.

[14] *The Seven Habits of Highly Effective People,* Covey, S, Simon & Schuster, 1989.

- Interpersonal skills – the more you demonstrate your ability to engage in positive conversations, the more you are admired by others and thus have an opportunity to exert influence.

- Flexibility and adaptability – similarly, the more you demonstrate your flexibility and adaptability, the more you will be admired by those on the receiving end of this trait.

- Commitment – the commitment you show to a cause, mission or personal value set is recognised and appreciated as showing integrity. Best described in management-speak as "walking the talk".

- Respect and trust – once again, the more you trust and respect others, the more you will be trusted and respected.

- Knowledge base and expertise – demonstrating your expertise and knowledge in the area you are trying to influence (which in many cases is in the area of interpersonal relationships, not task expertise) will enhance your expert power and your personal power.

- Wide network – especially in modern organisations, where having connections that help get things done for yourself and others is essential. Understanding and using the political influences (with a small "p") in organisations is an essential skill in getting results without authority.

USING YOUR POWER

Two other things need to be said about power and how you use it:

Firstly, power has the ability to be channelled either negatively or positively, and that decision is in the control of the user. You can choose to use your power to manipulate, put people down, bully or achieve your goals at the expense of others. Or you can choose to use power positively, to influence with integrity, to build relationships, seek win:win[15] solutions, support and challenge people positively, achieving both your goals and the other party's.

Secondly, power is rarely confined to one side in a relationship. Even the most downtrodden and powerless can hit back, disrupt or leave. The ability to influence is based on the balance of power, which is especially important in relationships where there is no position power - here the power balance starts out being even, often with one source of power offsetting another. And when it comes to estimating the balance of power, people very often underestimate the power they have and over-estimate the power of the other party. In deciding an influencing strategy, therefore, it is helpful to consider the sources of power that you and the other party have available, and seek to increase the balance of power in your favour.

So, from a perspective of getting results without authority and having a positive impact, personal power is the most effective. It is less likely to be perceived negatively, and can be very effective in tipping the balance of power. The potentially coercive impact of position power makes it the least effective. If you have position power, you need to be careful in its use so that its impact is not misunderstood.

---

[15] Definitions of terms used can be found in the Glossary at Appendix 1.

You also need to increase your skills in the breadth and depth of interpersonal communication to enhance your personal power.

The next chapter describes a model for analysing and applying influence methods to get what you want whilst building or maintaining the relationship between the parties. It will help to build flexibility, choice and skill in dealing with a wide range of situations and people in a positive way, including those where you have position power and wish to avoid its potential negative impact.

DEVELOPMENT EXERCISES

1. SOURCES OF POWER

- Consider all of the reasons that you do things for other people – how do they influence you? What sources of power do they use? How do you react to their approach – positively or negatively?

- Think of those whom you influence – what sources of power are you using? Where possible, check with these people to find whether your analysis is the same as theirs – are they perceiving you use a different power source?

- What position power do you hold? As a manager in a company? As a leader in a social or community group? As a parent? What is the impact on others of this position power?

2. DEVELOPING YOUR PERSONAL POWER

- Where can you increase your personal power? What can you do to enhance your interpersonal skills? What actions can you take to build trust and respect with others? What can you do to increase deposits into your 'emotional bank balance' that others hold?

PERSONAL SOURCES OF POWER & AUTHORITY

CHAPTER FOUR

KNOWING YOUR INFLUENCING PROFILE AND THAT OF OTHERS [16]

"Speaking the same language doesn't mean two people understanding each other."
YVES-NOËL DERENNE

"O wad some Power the giftie gie us
To see oursels as ithers see us!
It wad frae monie a blunder free us
An foolish notion:
What airs in dress an gait wad lea'es us,
An ev'n devotion!"
ROBERT BURNS, TO A LOUSE

You can enhance personal power by developing your interpersonal skills and your adaptability in the use of different ways to influence. This chapter describes the four influencing styles that you can use in situations. Each of the styles has a unique outcome, so you can make strategic choices regarding the style that will be most effective in getting what you want in a given situation. There is an

---

[16] Parts of this chapter were first published as *Influencing* by Geof Cox in *The Gower Handbook of Management, Fourth Edition,* D. Lock, ed., Gower, Aldershot, 1998. Reproduced with permission. From Gower.

exercise and a self-assessment diagnostic tool which will identify your own preferences in the use and reactions to the styles so that you can identify areas for further investigation and development.

WHAT INFLUENCE STYLES ARE AVAILABLE?

To start to understand the different possibilities and options there are to influence in a given situation, consider the following:

EXERCISE: PROJECT TEAM LEADER STYLE

Your company has decided to move its office to a new location. It has purchased a new building and all of the services are currently being installed. An announcement has been made to staff. The move is generally welcomed, as the existing office is small and overcrowded, and also has difficult transport arrangements. The new office is in a location with excellent transport and local services. There are of course those who do not wish to move - they are a minority, but influential group.

You are a member of a selection committee which must decide on the person criteria for a team leader for this project. You have a pool of candidates who are all technically qualified for the position. The project leader is expected to plan and carry out the relocation of all of the staff so that the business of the company is not interrupted. The project leader will be able to call on the time and expertise of a number of departmental coordinators to form a project planning and implementation team.

Which style do you believe will be most effective in this situation?

STYLE A

Is direct and positive in asserting their wishes and requirements. Lets others know what is wanted from them and is quick to tell them when pleased or dissatisfied. Will use their power and authority to get others to do what is wanted. Gets others to agree with plans and proposals and follows up to make sure people carry out their agreements. Has a strength in bargaining and negotiating, doing deals with others to get things done.

STYLE B

Is open and ready to admit to not having all of the answers. Listens attentively to the ideas and feelings of others, actively communicating interest in their contributions and understanding their points of view. Willing to be influenced by others whilst pursuing her or his own objectives. Gives support to others' ideas and accomplishments. Makes sure everyone is heard before a decision is made. Builds powerful and strong relationships with people by showing trust in others and helping to bring out their best abilities.

STYLE C

Appeals to the emotions and ideals of others through the use of forceful and colourful words and images. Projects an enthusiasm which is contagious. Brings people together by articulating a vision of future possibilities. Can see the exciting potential in an idea or situation and can communicate this excitement to others. Brings others to see the values, hopes and aspirations which they have in common and helps them to build these common values into a shared sense of loyalty and commitment.

STYLE D

Produces detailed and comprehensive proposals for dealing with problems. Finds and presents the logic behind ideas and is energetic in finding facts, arguments and opinions to support a position. Quick to grasp the strengths and weaknesses in an argument and to see and articulate the logical connections between different aspects of a complex situation. A determined defender of the logical approach to business problem solving.

What would be your preferred style or mix of styles for this appointment? What percentage would you allocate? 100% to one style? 50% to two styles? All four equally rated at 25%? Or some other split?

STYLE A		**STYLE C**	
STYLE B		**STYLE D**	

Your response to this question was probably based on two sets of data: your own personal comfort with the style described, and your experience of the requirements of managers in this sort of position. Whatever your preferred choice, it is possible to make a good case for any one of the styles to be effective in this position.

Style A will make the decisions necessary to keep to the deadlines and deliver the project. Style B would make sure that all of the potential pitfalls are identified and resolved, and that the minority are not ignored to the point of being destructive. Style C would also keep the minority on-side by inspiring them and the rest of the organisation to believe in the viability and need for the office move. Style D would deliver detailed and logical plans and schedules to make the project successful.

It is also possible to identify some potential pitfalls of each approach.

Style A would get things done quickly and would keep to the deadlines, but might antagonise and upset people. Style B would keep everyone happy and on-side, but runs the risk of opening up old issues and cause slippage and erosion of the project aims. Style C may also deliver the project on time, but could lose some of the detail focus with its emphasis on the big picture. Style D would stay calm and focused on data and rational analysis, but might get bogged down in detail and bureaucracy.

You have probably all seen these styles effectively and ineffectively used. For the project in this exercise, some balance of all four styles is probably the best choice for a good project manager, as all four styles are likely to be needed at some time to deliver the project effectively. Too much emphasis on one style might deliver some of the pitfalls, and not be effective for some of the objectives of the project.

A MODEL FOR EFFECTIVE INFLUENCING[17]

- *"When push comes to shove..."*
- *"Squeeze the lemons until the pips squeak."*

You hear people in organisations saying this when their first attempts to get results do not work. They are using (or inferring) position power, and increase pressure or force in order to achieve results. This may achieve a result, but it is only short lived, and will have a negative effect on the relationship. It is not, therefore, an appropriate way to get results, even if you have authority. If you do not have authority, it is even less likely to work.

Why do managers do this? The reason is an unhelpful, but natural response. When you try to change or influence

---

[17] The model and questionnaire used in this chapter were developed by Pierre Casse and first published in *Revisiting Communication: A 'new way' to manage it* in *The European Management Journal*, Vol. 12, No. 3, pages 253-8, September 1994. Reproduced with permission from Elsevier.

another person, you are using some form of energy – often a psychological energy, but one that is experienced similarly to physical energy. In business organisations, the most common energy used is pushing – directing your energy against or at the other person in order to get them to move in a particular direction, stop what they are doing or change. Managers issue directions or instructions, give orders, ask for reports and make proposals. Most of the time this works. It is an adult communication based on persuasion and acceptance of our respective roles. But it is pushing, and when you push against something, there is bound to be resistance.

When the resistance is such that the other party is not persuaded to take action – for instance, there may be strong vested interests, not enough information, or strong feelings – then the natural tendency is to push harder, to escalate the force. However the greater the force, the greater resistance (as Isaac Newton identified in his Laws of Motion!).

Luckily, there is a different way. You can try a different method of influencing, using a different energy and influence style to get what you want, and at the same time maintain your relationships or even enhance the relationships with the people you are influencing.

People tend to have a personal preference for using one or two of the styles. These would be styles that you find easy to use; styles that get you results most of the time; styles that you have been taught to use through school and training; styles that fit the cultures you live and work in; styles that fit your values and beliefs. (There is a self-assessment questionnaire later in this chapter which will identify your own preferences).

Someone who has been brought up to think and act in a logical and rational way and is working in an organisation that is practical and systematic in its approach is likely to use a rational approach to influencing, basing their interactions on facts, rules, procedures and logical argument. By contrast, someone who has been brought up to value and care about people and works in an organisation that is based on team work, self development and respect for the worth of the individual is likely to use a more people oriented approach to influencing, interacting more with feelings and emotions and seeking to understand.

If someone has strong tendencies in either of these directions, they will find it difficult to communicate effectively with someone from an opposite preference and therefore influence them. On the other hand, they will work effectively with people who share their mindset. In a tight, line management structure, different groups may exhibit similar characteristics – they have similar cultures and will have recruited people with traits that tend to fit. However, modern organisations and matrix/project structures bring together more cross functional dialogue and the opportunity for different preferences and cultures to clash. So, the more you can develop flexibility and adapt your style to meet the preference of the other party, the greater will be your capacity to influence.

In this model there are two main dimensions of behaviour in communication: the degree to which people are directive, and the degree to which people are responsive. People who are directive tend to be seen as more forceful and assertive, taking control, making quick decisions and take more risks. People who are responsive will be sensitive to, and willing to share, emotions and feelings, appear more friendly and are concerned about relationships. There are no absolutes in these two dimensions, as everyone is directive and responsive to some extent, but each will have a preference, a tendency to be more or less, which means you can effectively break down your influence patterns into four styles (see Figure 4-1).

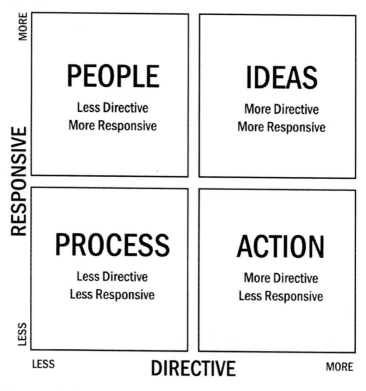

Figure 4-1: The four influencing styles

THE FOUR INFLUENCING STYLES[18]

ACTION STYLE

DESCRIPTION	PEOPLE TALK ABOUT:	PEOPLE ARE:
The action oriented mindset is fundamentally geared at changing things, improving existing situations, translating ideas into actions, being effective, getting things done, moving ahead and achieving good results. Outcome: *Deal*. Conversation style: *Bargaining*.	• Results • Objectives • Performance • Deals • Challenges • Moving ahead • Responsibility • Achievements • Change • Decisions	• Pragmatic • Direct • Impatient • Decisive • Quick • Energetic • Challenging

Action people are task-oriented, keen to get things done, decisive and direct. (More directive and less responsive). They use an energy that is *moving against* others, and can therefore be seen as forceful, pushy and aggressive if they overuse or misuse the approach. (This is Style A in the exercise earlier in the chapter).

They can moderate the strength of the push against you by moving from asking to demanding to indicate the importance of what they want done. But people using this style often just increase the pressure when they do

---

[18] A note on the names of the four styles – I am using the words "Action", "Process", "People" and "Ideas" to describe four different ways of communicating. Readers should not take the names too literally. For instance, using the word 'idea' in conversation does not mean the person is using the Ideas style. You can present an 'idea' in any of the four styles. This is particularly important for readers who are not native English speakers; literal translation of the words may infer a different meaning.

not get the response they want, and end up in a domineering stance. For Action style people, the end often justifies the means.

However, used well, the results focus and urgency to get things done are very motivational. They balance the demands they make on others with rewards and incentives to construct deals that are fair and balanced: *"You do this for me, I will do this for you."*

CASE STUDY: THE GOOD BANKER

Frank was the chief executive of a major bank (one that emerged from the 2008/9 financial crisis without having to be bailed out by vast sums of Government money). He was very focused on targets and results – the performance of the bank was paramount. But he also used his direct style to make some significant changes in the management style of the bank. He replaced the "results at any cost" mentality with a culture that was focused on not just *what* you achieved, but on *how* you achieved it. To show he meant it, he also allocated 50% of the annual salary and bonus budget to reward appropriate behaviour – the how – thus moving away from the traditional focus on financial results only.

He also made it very clear to his senior managers that they needed to "walk the talk" and demonstrate this change in the way they managed their teams. It was an essential change to the long term performance of the bank (as later events clearly showed) and he needed the commitment of his management team. As a result, several senior managers left the company. The deal was either you are in or you are out. They left with good financial packages and most went immediately into other jobs with other companies. They could not make the change, and the choice for them was made very clear.

For those managers who did remain, there was clarity on

---

the objectives to be followed – in both the what (financial performance) and the how (behaviour). Measures of success were put in place, and a coaching style of management provided a supportive structure to help make the changes happen. It became easy for managers to translate the overall goals for the bank into individual objectives for members of staff as they were direct and simply worded. They were able to easily craft objectives for day to day activities, and link those clearly to the financial and other rewards on offer. Frank had confidence that his staff, worldwide, wanted to contribute and make a difference to the bank if only they knew how. By providing the clarity on performance and results, he created this clear line of sight through his effective use of Action style. He gave a focus that people could believe in, not one that was solely self-serving for the bank shareholders, but one where all of the bank employees knew how to create and share in success.

PROCESS STYLE

DESCRIPTION	PEOPLE TALK ABOUT:	PEOPLE ARE:
The process oriented mindset is characterised by the need to know, be factual, understand, organise, structure, set up strategies, tactics, establish rules, regulations, systems and manage. Outcome: *Solution*. Conversation style: *Debating*.	• Facts • Details • Observations • Procedures • Planning • Proof • Organising • Controlling • Testing • Analysis	• Systematic • Logical • Factual • Verbose • Unemotional • Cautious • Patient

Process style people also use a pushing type of energy, but are less directive and forceful, relying more on the logical and rational nature of their argument, *moving at* the other party in order to reach a solution. Overuse or misuse of this style results in inflexible sets of rules and procedures, bureaucracy and verbosity. It is a favourite style of communication for many people and for business, especially as the first resort. (This is Style D in the exercise).

Often found in large organisations and especially in the public sector, this style of communication relies on due process to make decisions, thus mitigating against the potential abuse of power that could be used by someone in a hierarchical position in the organisation. Authority is limited by a set of rules, policies and procedures that determine how decisions are made, often in some form of committee or team structure. The focus of Process style is to leverage the specialist knowledge, experience and data available to find the best way forward, based on proven methods and systems.

The potential to minimise risk makes it a favourite approach in managers who are cautious and patient, working in organisations where the right answer is more important than the speed of the decision. It is a style that is grounded in the scientific method and in root cause analysis. The danger in this style is in the tendency to over-elaborate, over-organise and over-control. It is difficult to change direction and decision making is slow. And in times of rapid change in the environment, gathering and analysing historic data to decide the way forward becomes a little like trying to play tennis by watching the scoreboard.

CASE STUDY: THE ENGINEERING MANAGER

Dennis was an engineering manager in a major oil company. He was a keen observer of all things physical, making daily tours of the facility to inspect the pipe-work, tanks, valves, boilers, controls and safety systems. He would notice if something was wrong based on his years of experience and knowledge of the engineering technology. He had an eye for the potential problem.

After each of his morning tours, he convened a meeting of his management team. Using a standard agenda they reviewed the plans for the day's activities, making sure that everything was in place and coordinated. They reviewed known future customer demands and maintenance activities, then discussed and planned for the required shut-downs and production. Guesswork was not permitted; if some information was not available, a decision was delayed until the facts were available. The final plans were summarised on a board on display to the whole plant, so everyone knew what was happening.

The inherent danger in the products they handled placed a strong emphasis on safety. Dennis himself chaired a monthly safety committee composed of representatives from all levels and from all areas of the operation. This committee looked at potential hazards, collected and analysed data and proposed changes to physical layouts and procedures in order to improve safety. If there was any form of incident, committee members were despatched to investigate and gather observed information from the people involved and the surrounding environment, in order to ensure that a similar occurrence could not happen again.

They were so successful in improving the safety of the plant that there were months, then years between accidents. Then, instead of declaring the safety problem solved, they turned their attention to investigate near-accidents and potential incidents with the same vigour and became the industry leader.

Dennis's Process style was uniquely suited to the situation. He used his systematic, calm, unemotional approach to create one of the most efficient, safe and cost effective plants in the industry.

PEOPLE STYLE

DESCRIPTION	PEOPLE TALK ABOUT:	PEOPLE ARE:
The people oriented mindset is characterised by men and women who care about people, have a strong drive towards people's needs, rights, communication, understanding each other, team-work, ethics, synergy, feelings and emotions. Outcome: *Understanding*. Conversation style: *Empathetic*.	• People • Needs • Self development • Sensitivity • Relationships • Motivations • Beliefs • Values • Awareness • Co-operation • Communications • Feelings • Team spirit • Understanding	• Spontaneous • Empathetic • Warm • Subjective • Emotional • Perceptive • Sensitive

The People style uses listening and sharing to help people to build understanding. The energy used is *moving with*, using the energy of the other person in a positive way to develop a relationship and to influence, not to manipulate or dominate. The mindset of people orientation is characterised by a strong desire towards teamwork, synergy, communication and the needs of others. It is empathetic and sensitive. (This is Style B in the exercise).

At its best, People style leads to a highly participative management style where people feel as though they are important and their contribution is valued. It is typified in two quotations from the Chinese Taoist philosopher Lao-Tzu who lived in the 5th Century BC[19]:

> *"The highest type of ruler is one of whose existence the people are barely aware. Next comes one whom they love and praise. Next comes one whom they fear. Next comes one whom they despise and defy. When you are lacking in faith, others will be unfaithful to you. The Sage is self-effacing and scanty of words."*

> *"Go to the people. Learn from them. Live with them. Start with what they know. Build with what they have. But of the best leaders, when his task is accomplished and things have been completed, the people will say, 'We have done it ourselves!' "*

People style is also the foundation to the servant leadership approach pioneered by Robert K. Greenleaf: the idea that the best leaders are servants first, wanting to bring value by lifting up others and doing what supports the greater good for all. This is sharply different from those who see themselves as leaders first, motivated by the need for power, prestige and/or material rewards[20].

At its worst, People style can put good relations before task completion, and create a major barrier to action with every single decision requiring consensus. It can also lead to the phenomenon of "groupthink" where group members try to minimise conflict and reach consensus without critically testing, analysing, and evaluating ideas. Group cohesiveness is paramount and members of the group avoid promoting viewpoints outside the comfort zone of consensus thinking. As a result groups tend to

---

[19] Lao Tzu, Tao Te Ching
[20] The Greenleaf Center for Servant Leadership, http://www.greenleaf.org

make hasty, irrational decisions, where individual doubts which may be valid are set aside, for fear of upsetting the group's balance.

CASE STUDY: SERVANT LEADERSHIP

Jack was the founder of a plumbing and air conditioning company in Dallas, Texas. He was an early reader (in the early 1970s) of the essay by Robert K. Greenleaf "The Servant as Leader" and ordered hundreds of copies of the essay to distribute throughout his company.

He started to redistribute the decision making in the company and trained all the employees in the mindset and skills of servant leadership. Supervisors worked hard on creating high performance teams synergising the collective intelligence of the team members and focusing on performance.

Putting the servant leadership into action himself, Jack shared some of his ideas for the future of the company – one that recognised the unique contribution that the employees could make, if they were given the opportunity. They could work together to grow the company. He encouraged the supervisors and managers to coach and develop people rather than give directions or discipline. Jack led by example by building the confidence and competence in his immediate management team. He found that the more he showed faith in them, believed in them and gave them opportunities, the more they rose to the occasion.

He took time to listen to the people in the organisation, find out their aspirations. He put himself in their shoes and helped them make their dreams come true (which, at the same time, made his company stronger and more successful).

Now, more than thirty years after reading the essay, the company has over 900 employees who also own 75% of the

---

stock in the company. It is consistently recognised as one of Fortune Magazine's *"100 Best Companies to Work For In America"* since the list started in 1995 and is often ranked in the top ten.

Jack used the People style to great effect, and has left the legacy of this culture to his successors. Far from being paralysed by consensus decision making and a focus on relationship before task, the company is highly successful and performance focused. As well as being a "Best Company" to work for, it is also financially sound and continues to grow.

IDEAS STYLE

DESCRIPTION	PEOPLE TALK ABOUT:	PEOPLE ARE:
The ideas oriented people handle the world in terms of concepts, abstractions, theories and models. They value imagination, innovation and creativity very much. They are future oriented. Outcome: *Cooperation.* Conversation style: *Inspiring.*	• Concepts • Innovation • Creativity • Potential • Opportunities • Possibilities • Grand designs • Improving • Interdependence • What's new in the field • Alternatives	• Imaginative • Charismatic • Difficult to understand • Ego-centred • Unrealistic • Creative • Full of ideas • Provocative

Ideas style uses responsiveness to connect with other people's values and beliefs and to build exciting possibilities for the future. Outcomes of cooperation are achieved through *moving together* with the people they are trying to influence. This style is dependent on personal, and sometimes expert, power rather than position or resource power. However, the position one holds may give more of an opportunity to exercise the style in the context of leadership. It is a style that does not try to influence by pushing people into action, but by attracting, or pulling them. (This is Style C in the exercise).

People using Ideas style effectively cut through bureaucracy and red tape, boldly following the goal or vision that they have and inspire others to join them in the quest. They are invariably positive thinkers, looking forward to future opportunities and full of ideas. However, without the firm foundation of some common ground with a critical mass of others, their ideas stay just as ideas. The style is not effective unless they can resonate with others who can share their ideals and work together to deliver the future.

CASE STUDY: THE PROJECT MANAGER

Pauline was a project manager in an IT company. She was charged with delivering new applications to a diverse customer base with a team of people drawn from different functions, often in different physical locations. As is normal in project based organisations, she could expect that all of the team would be working on other projects and tasks at the same time. She had no position power to make people work on her project rather than the others for which they were responsible. The only solution was to get her project team members to believe that her projects were the most important and most interesting, so that they would automatically look to contribute to her project first.

In doing this, Pauline was an expert. Whenever a new project was in the planning stage, she would imagine the impact that the new application would have on the company, its customers, and the users. She would also imagine the project from the perspectives of the cross functional team who would be working on the project with her. How could she inspire each and every one of them?

Then she would take time with each new team member to emphasise the common values and desires they both had. For engineers and technical specialists, it was the desire to create something that was technically excellent and innovative. For sales staff, it was to create something that really enhanced the user experience. For planners and finance staff, she highlighted the aspiration of being associated with delivering a project ahead of time and under budget. With each individual, she made a strong connection so that they were working to similar values and goals.

On the back of these strong connections, Pauline could then share her vision and ideas for the new application. She would paint a word picture of what the success would feel like for each of the team members, in their own language. Her enthusiasm and commitment and the realisation that it could also deliver each person's own aspirations, would inspire them to want to work with Pauline. With a record of creating a strong team and a collective enthusiasm to deliver, it was then easy for Pauline to influence her senior managers to give her the sole responsibility for the project, thus minimising any outside interference and unnecessary reporting.

Without fail, Pauline's projects were delivered on time, on budget, with some of the best technical innovation. They were also commercially successful as users found them both functional and easy to operate.

YOUR INFLUENCING ARENA

Knowing your own preferred style and that of others helps you to map your influencing arena – the environment in which you operate. At the end of this chapter there is a self-assessment questionnaire that will help you to identify your own preference and values in communicating with others. Observation and reflection on actual conversations is just as valid. Take notice of how you communicate with others and how they communicate with you. Most people will use a mix of styles in normal life, but will have a preference for the use of one or two styles, and use these most of the time. Some of the use of style may be positive, some negative. Either is an observation of the use of the style.

What style do others that you work with typically use? What style do you typically use? Refer to the style descriptions above to get some clues and also to reflect on the following style traits:

ACTION STYLE

- I say exactly what I want.
- I make clear my demands and expectations.
- I am impatient.
- I offer to make a deal.
- I commit to do something in return for my demands.
- I am willing to give something in order to get something.

PROCESS STYLE

- I put forward proposals and suggestions.
- I present clearly and calmly.
- I propose solutions.
- I use facts to support my ideas.
- I am systematic and logical.
- I argue against opposing points of view.

PEOPLE STYLE

- I share information about my personal feelings.
- I express my hopes and fears.
- I ask for help when uncertain or confused.
- I test understanding of what others have said.
- I ask questions to seek more information.
- I draw others out to fully understand their concerns.

IDEAS STYLE

- I identify common goals and values.
- I establish common ground with others.
- I emphasise areas of agreement.
- I communicate optimism and enthusiasm.
- I share my ambitions and dreams.
- I focus on future possibilities.

You can plot where people are in your Influencing Arena below.

Figure 4-2: Your Influencing Arena

CULTURAL DIFFERENCES IN STYLE PREFERENCE

Our preferences are affected by a number of influences – our education, upbringing, role models, parents, profession, gender, age, and nationality. These all go together to build up a strong identity of "how I do things." Cluster people together who have similar identities, and you have a culture, whether that be a national culture; a professional culture such as sales or engineering or accountancy; an organisation culture (this is the way we do things around here); or one that is age or generation related. These different cultures have often developed a way of communicating and influencing that suits them, and this then has an impact in your influencing arena whenever you cross a barrier and try to work with someone from a different culture.

Crossing these frontiers or barriers is commonplace now with a global workforce that spans national boundaries and project working where operating in cross functional teams is natural. Understanding different cultures helps to get better results through being able to adapt to the needs and preferences of the different culture.

A preference to Action-oriented communication can be identified in the USA, Canada, Australia and other nationalities where action and speed are of the essence. Organisations that rely on short term decision making – fast moving consumer goods, sales, and retail – will probably have a preference towards Action style. Many senior managers in organisations also tend to use this style as organisations notice and promote people who seem to get results. Many performance related reward systems reinforce a preference for Action style with a focus on target achievement over relationship management.

Process-oriented communication is preferred in cultures where structure and logical decision making are paramount. Countries such as Austria, Germany, Denmark, and Sweden come immediately to mind. Professions such as technology, engineering and accountancy where there is a strong reliance on a scientific and systematic methodology use Process style. Process driven organisations – oil and chemicals, pharmaceuticals, engineering, manufacturing, and government – all rely on solid, data driven problem solving, and will exhibit strong Process style tendencies. Process style communication is also predominant in the way we are taught in schools, so it has a comfortable feel, even if it is not your individual preference.

People-oriented communication is the cultural norm in countries where consensus and respect for people and their ideas is important, e.g. Asia, and Japan. In this culture, the relationship is more significant than the task, so it can also be identified in social science driven professions such as social work, human resources, health and education (primarily at the delivery point rather than in the management, which accounts for some of the difficult relationships in these professions between practitioners and managers).

Ideas-oriented communication is typical of cultures where it is the norm to ask questions like "What are the arguments for doing it this way? Why? Why not?" because people must be convinced of the substance in the message being conveyed. This is common in countries like France and in research and development and project leadership. It is a style that is attractive to some of the younger generations where they want to believe in what they are doing and in the purpose behind the organisation, not just to do a job.

YOUR PREFERRED INFLUENCING STYLE

In the following self-assessment questionnaire[21], select one of the statements in each pair of attributes which is most typical of your personality. No pair is an either–or proposal, so some of the choices are more difficult than others. For the best results, answer honestly, and make your choice as spontaneously as possible. Don't try to answer how you think you should answer, or how you would like to appear. There is no "right" or "wrong" answer.

- ❑ 1. I like action.
- ❑ 2. I deal with problems in a systematic way.

- ❑ 3. I like to attend well-organised meetings.
- ❑ 4. Deadlines are important to me.

- ❑ 5. I do not like hesitation.
- ❑ 6. I believe that new ideas have to be tested before being used.

- ❑ 7. I want to set my own objectives.
- ❑ 8. When I start something I stay with it until the end.

- ❑ 9. I look forward to receiving feedback on my performance.
- ❑ 10. I find a step-by-step approach very effective.

- ❑ 11. Planning is the key to success.
- ❑ 12. I become impatient with long discussions.

- ❑ 13. I believe that teams are more effective than individuals.
- ❑ 14. I value experience very much.

- ❑ 15. I enjoy working with people.
- ❑ 16. I like to handle several projects at the same time.

- ❑ 17. I enjoy the stimulation of interaction with others.
- ❑ 18. I learn by doing.

---

[21] This questionnaire was developed by Pierre Casse of INSEAD and first published in *Revisiting Communication: A 'new way' to manage it* in *The European Management Journal, Vol. 12, No. 3, pages 253-8, September 1994.* Reproduced with permission from Elsevier.

❑ 19. I try to understand other peoples' emotions.
❑ 20. I see myself as decisive.

❑ 21. I think I am good at reading people.
❑ 22. I seek challenging tasks.

❑ 23. I am sensitive to others' needs.
❑ 24. I like to achieve.

❑ 25. I listen to people.
❑ 26. I like variety.

❑ 27. I enjoy innovation very much.
❑ 28. I am impatient with long, slow assignments.

❑ 29. I am more interested in the future than in the past.
❑ 30. I usually make decisions without thinking too much.

❑ 31. I am always looking for new possibilities.
❑ 32. I like to get things done.

❑ 33. I challenge people around me.
❑ 34. I am impulsive.

❑ 35. I like creative problem solving.
❑ 36. I usually jump from one task to another.

❑ 37. I dream and think of possibilities all the time.
❑ 38. I dislike wasting my time.

❑ 39. People say that I am a fast thinker.
❑ 40. I like brief, to the point statements.

❑ 41. I am calm under pressure.
❑ 42. I like to co-operate with others.

❑ 43. I use logical methods to test alternatives.
❑ 44. I can predict how others may react to a certain action.

❑ 45. I believe that my head rules my heart.
❑ 46. I am able to assess the climate of a group.

❑ 47. Analysis should always come before action,
❑ 48. I can express my feelings openly.

❑ 49. I rely on my observations and data to make decisions,
❑ 50. I see myself as a good communicator.

- ❏ 51. I like to focus on one issue at a time.
- ❏ 52. I enjoy learning about others.

- ❏ 53. Facts speak for themselves.
- ❏ 54. I strongly believe that people need each other to get work done.

- ❏ 55. Key decisions have to be made in a cautious way.
- ❏ 56. I always question myself.

- ❏ 57. Emotions create problems.
- ❏ 58. I do not like details.

- ❏ 59. I tend to start things and not finish them.
- ❏ 60. I believe in a scientific approach.

- ❏ 61. I like to design new projects.
- ❏ 62. I accept differences in people.

- ❏ 63. I enjoy reading very much.
- ❏ 64. I like to organise.

- ❏ 65. I use my imagination as much as possible.
- ❏ 66. I enjoy doing what I am good at.

- ❏ 67. My brain never stops working.
- ❏ 68. I am impatient with details.

- ❏ 69. I like to be liked by others.
- ❏ 70. I can make deductions very quickly.

- ❏ 71. I try out my new ideas on people.
- ❏ 72. Good relationships are essential.

- ❏ 73. Communicating with people does not need a purpose.
- ❏ 74. I like to be intellectually stimulated.

- ❏ 75. Talking and working with people is a creative act.
- ❏ 76. Living by my own values and beliefs is key for me.

- ❏ 77. I enjoy playing with ideas.
- ❏ 78. I learn by interacting with others.

- ❏ 79. I find concepts and ideas interesting and enjoyable.
- ❏ 80. I feel confident in myself.

SCORING

In the matrix below, circle the items you have selected and add them up, giving one point for each item chosen. The maximum mark for any style is 20 and the total of the four styles should be 40.

ACTION			PROCESS			PEOPLE			IDEAS		
1	4	5	2	3	6	13	15	17	27	29	31
7	9	12	8	10	11	19	21	23	33	35	37
14	16	18	41	43	45	25	42	44	39	56	58
20	22	24	47	49	51	46	48	50	59	61	63
26	28	30	53	55	57	52	54	69	65	67	70
32	34	36	60	62	64	72	73	75	71	74	76
	38	40		66	68		78	80		77	79
Total			Total			Total			Total		

INTERPRETING THE RESULTS

A score between 1 and 7 in any style shows a somewhat underdeveloped and/or underused style. You have difficulty interacting with people who are strong in that category. Natural misunderstanding will occur, communication breakdown will take place and you will have a tendency to pass negative value judgements on each other and reject each other.

A score between 8 and 15 shows a well developed and/or used style, and generally shows a certain degree of flexibility and adaptability. People with an equal profile (10, 10, 10, 10) are quite good at adjusting to different people, situations and requirements. The problem may be that they are sometimes too good at switching and can then be perceived as being unpredictable.

A score between 16 and 20 shows a somewhat overdeveloped and/or overused style, generally characterised by a need to impose their values, beliefs and assumptions on others. People can be trapped into only one way of looking at things and are often biased and rigid.

People who have the same dominant mindset tend to get along very well.

DEVELOPMENT EXERCISES

1. YOUR PERSONAL STYLE

- Complete the self-assessment questionnaire.
- What are the strengths and weaknesses of your preferred style balance? Where do you score high? What is the impact of this? Where do you score low? What is the impact?
- Do you notice that you are using different styles in different situations and with different people? What is the impact of this?

2. YOUR INFLUENCING ARENA

- What are the preferred styles of your immediate influence targets: Your boss? Your colleagues? Your direct reports? Your senior managers? Your matrix/ project colleagues? Your business partners? Use the style descriptions to identify their most used approach.
- What are the implications of your preferred style and theirs? Where possible get feedback from your colleagues on the impact of your communication with them. Find out what they would identify as ways of improving your communication with them.
- Where you have a difficult relationship in your influencing arena, is there a clash of preferred styles? What could you do to change your approach to make a positive impact?
- Can you identify different cultures in your influencing arena where a department, function, national, age or professional group seem to exhibit similar preferred ways of communication? What is the impact of this on you?

CHAPTER FIVE

THE IMPACT OF EMOTION

"Suppose we were able to share meanings freely without a compulsive urge to impose our view or to conform to those of others and without distortion and self-deception. Would this not constitute a real revolution in culture?"

DAVID BOHM

"The greatest discovery of our generation is that human beings can alter their lives by altering their attitudes of mind. As you think, so shall you be."

WILLIAM JAMES

Emotions and feelings affect the way we all behave. We would like to think that all of our behaviour is rational, but just think for a moment about what drives you to do certain things – you want to be loved, you are afraid of looking stupid or bad in front of others, you fear being excluded, you want to be successful... all of these drivers are emotional. Then, seemingly instantaneously, rational thought processes kick in to develop strategies so that we avoid our fears and achieve our needs. The outcome is that we believe we are behaving rationally, when in fact we are being driven emotionally.

This chapter explores how your emotions and feelings can prevent you getting the result you want; how your communications can often be misinterpreted and misunderstood; and you will discover some tools that will help you to have a more positive and controlled impact in your relationships with others.

MIXED MESSAGES

- *You watch someone giving a talk, and you don't believe what they are saying.*

- *You are in conversation with someone, and you find yourself thinking that they are hiding something from you.*

- *Your child returns from school, tells you the day was OK, but you are certain that something is upsetting them.*

- *Despite protestations to the contrary, you are sure that your friend is concerned about something.*

These are all common situations where we don't believe what we are being told. How do you know? Where do you get the clues that all is not well?

There may be some factual information that you can point to – the speaker in the talk may have used some data that you know, conclusively, to be incorrect. But most likely the majority of your judgement is coming not from what the person is actually saying, but from the way they are saying it. There is something in the tone of their voice or their facial expressions that cause you to question what you hear. Sometimes, the information you get from these non-verbal clues is so strong that it over-rides completely the factual data that you are hearing them speak. You switch off completely from the content and focus entirely on the non-verbal messages. When you get mixed messages between what you hear and what you feel, then you tend to believe what you feel.

If this is what is happening to the way you listen to others, then the same process applies with people who are listening to you. If you are going to be able to influence someone, you need to make sure that they are not receiving a mixed message.

NON-VERBAL COMMUNICATION

Non-verbal communication is simply communication without words. At the extreme, a mime artist or ballet dancer is conveying the whole meaning through non-verbal communication. But in most situations, non-verbal communication is an amplifier of – or detractor from – the spoken word.

The whole gambit of non-verbal communication includes gesture and touch, facial expressions, eye contact, body language, posture, dress, clothing, spatial distance, physical appearance, and the rhythm, intonation, stress and tone of the voice. A lot to take in and understand whilst you are simultaneously processing the content of the verbal message!

You are able to process this wealth of information and make judgements, often sub-consciously, partly because you learn to use and understand non-verbal communication long before you learn the verbal skills. Babies learn to interpret non-verbal messages shortly after birth and young children are generally more adept at reading nonverbal cues than adults. This is due, in part, to their limited verbal skills – they know far more than they can verbalise and therefore rely on the non-verbal to communicate. Then, as they develop verbal skills, the non-verbal channels of communication become a part of the total communication process, but now mostly at the sub-conscious level.

Adults consciously use non-verbal communication because they recognise that words alone have limitations. There are many times when gesture is more effective than a verbal explanation. Try describing a spiral staircase without using your hands, or giving someone directions in the street! What they don't realise a lot of the time is that the signals they give non-verbally are powerful as they express inner feelings and thoughts, and cannot be controlled as easily as spoken words. This is where people typically come unstuck and send mixed messages which undermine their influence. They control the words they are speaking, but send a different message with their non-verbal communication.

THE WORDS, MUSIC & DANCE OF COMMUNICATION

A famous, but not universally applicable (in his own words), piece of research by Albert Mehrabian[22] found that clues from spoken words, from the voice tone, and from the facial expression contribute 7%, 38%, and 55% respectively to the total meaning of a message. Obviously, it depends on the context – you do not understand 93% of the message of someone speaking in a foreign language. But there are some important points embedded in this, and other research:

- when communicating person-to-person, much of the meaning is communicated verbally, and much is communicated non-verbally

- a lot of communication is carried out non-verbally

- when we are communicating feelings and attitude, the non-verbal messages are more significant (this was the focus of Mehrabian's research)

- we are less conscious of the de-coding of non-verbal information

- when we are unsure about the content and when we trust the other person less, we pay more attention to what we hear and see

---

[22] Mehrabian, A. (1971). *Silent Messages*, Wadsworth, California: Belmont

- when we do not have the non-verbal clues, the chances of misunderstanding the communication is higher

Figure 5-1: The Words, Music and Dance of communication

So, to return to the situations posed at the start of this section: the chances are that you picked up messages from the Music (the tone of voice and intonation of how these words are spoken) and the Dance (the gestures, posture, eye contact and body language) which did not match the Words (their literal meaning). When there is a mixed message people will tend to believe the Music and Dance not the Words.

Why does this happen? One reason is that you decode messages in the brain at different levels and at different speeds. Your response to a lot of body language is instantaneous and unconscious. It triggers a built-in, automatic response mechanism to keep you from danger and to survive. Body language triggers a reaction in the "oldest" part of the brain, often referred to as the reptilian brain. This has a primary responsibility to keep you alive and reproducing. So messages conveying possible aggression or gestures conveying attraction will have an immediate impact. And this then affects what happens next in decoding. Before you hear the words, or have a chance to try to understand them, you are already reacting to the other person, and that is affecting your judgement.

The next level of the brain is often referred to as the limbic system. It is the emotional brain, also called the mammalian brain as we share its functions with other mammals who can convey emotion. It helps to guide you towards pleasurable activities and away from harmful ones that you have learned through experience. So when you hear a voice tone that you connect with past experience, you link into the emotional brain and what you know of the feelings and emotions that these bring. You have now made up your mind about the context in which you will interpret what the other person is saying.

The final interpretation takes place in the largest and most complex level of the brain, the neo-cortex. This is the thinking part of the brain you share with other human beings. It is what makes us who you are: the ability to use complex language, logic, reasoning and other higher level processes. So you tend to believe that this is the dominant part of the brain. But, by the time you expend effort in the neo-cortex working out the language of the complex message, you have already made up your mind whether you believe the other person or not, whether you like them or not, and whether they are a threat to you or not – and a lot of subtlety in between. You decode the message in this context. Your emotions and feelings have controlled your decision. (As shown in Figure 5-2)

Figure 5-2: Sequence of decoding a message

The double-whammy comes when you send a message, as shown in Figure 5-3. When you think about sending an important message or making a presentation, you probably spend the majority of the time writing the script (words). If you have time left, and if it is really important you may read through the presentation to make sure you say it right (music) – though surprisingly few of us will say the words out loud, and even fewer will rehearse with someone else in order to get feedback. Finally, a tiny number will consider their posture or body language – most will just turn up on the day and deliver their presentation cold.

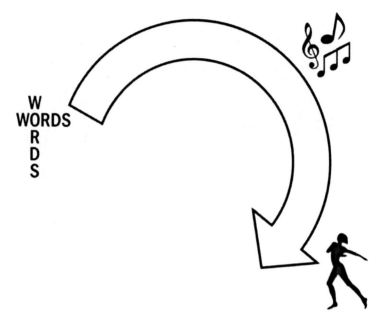

Figure 5-3: Sequence for coding a message

No wonder there is so much miscommunication. We should take more notice of the acting profession, who spend days and weeks rehearsing the words, music and dance to make sure that their message is believable by their audience.

OPPORTUNITIES FOR MISCOMMUNICATION

Think about the messages you send, and the messages you receive. Recall some situations where you received a mixed message, and identify what it was in the other person's behaviour – the Words, Music or Dance – that caused you to question the message you received. Also think about the messages you are sending, unconsciously, to others through your Music and Dance. Are you sending mixed messages?

Also reflect that the opportunity for miscommunication increases when you are not face to face with the other person. If you cannot see the other person (for instance when you are on the telephone), then you are missing out on the clues you both send and pick up from the Dance. There is more of an opportunity to misunderstand the other person, and to be misunderstood yourself without these visual clues. You will often be more aware of the vocal clues – you can hear someone smile in their voice tone – but you will still be making judgements on less than perfect data.

When you then consider that a massive amount of your influence and communication takes place electronically through emails, the opportunity to send or receive a miscommunication grows enormously. You are relying on Words alone. Yes, it is possible to bring in tone to writing, but not to the extent of hearing and seeing the other person. And bringing tone into writing usually involves longer sentences and explanations – but email and instant messaging practice tends to reduce the length of messages. How easy is it to get the wrong idea from an email? It is so easy that a new communication medium has been created– the "emoticon". You put a smiley at the end of a message to make sure people know that you are making a joke and to not take it seriously.

So, non-verbal communication creates a massive opportunity for miscommunication. Once again the impact you have may be different from your intent. You need to continually check to make sure that the message you are sending is being received the way you intended. You can pick up clues by observing the receiver and checking that the reaction is what you expected. And you can make sure that the messages you send are congruent in their Words, Music and Dance so that you minimise the potential for a mixed message. Later chapters look in detail at each of the four influencing styles, so you can identify the Words, Music and Dance of each and practise being congruent and effective.

THE LADDER OF INFERENCE

Another area where our feelings and emotions can cause problems is in the routines that you set up to protect yourself from the fears you have, and to manage the overwhelming amount of data you have to process every second.

It is impossible to live without having some routines and drawing conclusions from what you see and hear. But some of these routines may also create impediments. They lead you to misinterpret signals, distort the data you observe to fit your reality, and even reject valid information because it does not fit with your own belief system. One way to describe this process was developed by Harvard Professor Chris Argyris: The Ladder of Inference[23].

The ladder is a way to examine how we all think (see Figure 5-4). It shows how you limit your thinking affected by the context so that you make assumptions and value judgements that are coloured by your past experiences of the context, your beliefs, and your attitudes.

---

[23] *Overcoming Organizational Defences*, Chris Argyris, Allyn & Bacon, Needham, MA, 1990; also Rick Ross in *The Fifth Discipline Fieldbook*, Eds. Peter Senge, et al, Nicholas Brearley, London, 1994.

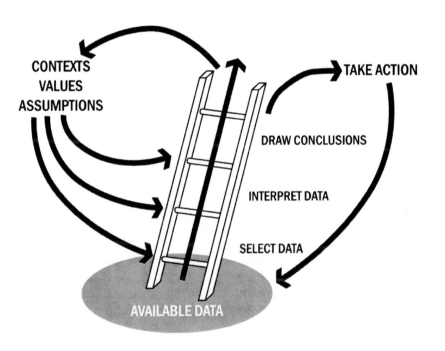

Figure 5-4: The Ladder of Inference

Take this simple example to see how the ladder works in practice:

> *You see a skinhead youth running down a street towards a business man carrying a briefcase (selecting some of the data from the scene playing out in front of you). You analyse and make sense of that data by relating to what you already know and have experienced in such situations, and interpret it to mean that the youth is about to steal the businessman's case. This assumption is reinforced by the businessman then holding his briefcase close to his chest. You draw a conclusion that skinhead youths are not to be trusted and will seek to rob you at any time, and will act accordingly when you see another skinhead youth in the street.*

> *If, however, you took a wider view of the scene, you might notice as well that a builder's hoist directly above the businessman was broken, and a ton of bricks was about to fall on him. The skinhead youth was in fact running towards the businessman to pull him out of the way and save his life. If you had chosen to select more data from the pool of available data on offer to you in the scene, you would make a different interpretation, draw a different conclusion and take different actions in the future.*[24]

Why might you interpret the original data negatively? Probably because of what has been written in the media, your own experiences, what you have heard. These beliefs form the contexts in which you then observe future situations, and what data you choose to select. The values you hold and the assumptions you make will affect the way you interpret that information and the conclusions you then make feed and strengthen the assumptions. You will then

---

[24] This story is taken from a famous TV advert for The Guardian newspaper 'Points of View' which can be viewed at www.youtube.com/watch?v=E3h-T3KQNxU

actively seek to find data to support your conclusion. We all have a self-generating cycle which, if negative, leads to prejudice, stereotyping and blinkered thinking.

People are so skilled at this form of thinking that they jump up the ladder without realising. They jump to conclusions very easily, and they believe them implicitly. The strength of this process can be seen in police files where eye witnesses to a crime have totally different recollections of what happened. Because of the way people think, they register some data and ignore other data, they interpret the data based on their previously held assumptions, values and contexts, and the outcome is a firm conclusion that is so obvious and clear to them that they see no need to think about how they reached that decision. They have reached the "truth". Someone else selects different data, interprets that in their context, come to a different conclusion and has also reached the "truth".

In the context of getting results and influencing someone, understanding this thinking process is invaluable. On a large number of occasions, differences and disagreements are based on different interpretations and conclusions drawn from a common pool of data. But instead of reaching down to try to understand each other, we tend to stand at the top of our respective ladders and hurl conclusions at each other. It then makes it harder to resolve the differences and reach a solution.

A strategic approach to getting results in situations of disagreement is to engage in a process of inquiry and advocacy. That way you can surface the differences in the conclusions you have each reached and find a way to create a different conclusion.

INQUIRY AND ADVOCACY

To do this successfully, you must resist the temptation to push your own conclusions even more forcefully – to persuade the other person that they are "wrong" – and first **inquire** into the other person's reasoning, assumptions, values, beliefs and data. What you are essentially doing is helping them to move back down their Ladder of Inference by questioning and showing genuine interest in understanding where they are coming from. This approach is the same as Steven Covey's Habit 5 from his bestseller, the 7 Habits of Highly Effective People[25]: "Seek First to Understand, Then to be Understood."

Once you have put in the effort to understand, then you can come back up the Ladder of Inference on your side, by **advocating** your opinion – starting with the data you selected, how and why you interpreted it the way you did in order to reach your different conclusion. As you listened to the other's argument first, and suspended your judgement, then the other party will be more positively disposed to listen to your advocacy, especially if it is built up and not just delivered as another "obvious truth" conclusion. This of course requires skills in effective listening and good advocacy (which will be covered in more detail in the next chapter).

The objective in inquiry and advocacy is not to try to convince the other party of the correctness of your position, or manipulate the other into agreement with you. The objective is to seek to find a common data set which you can then interpret together using agreed assumptions and values, in order to reach a new conclusion and solution. It takes time, effort and no small amount of patience, but the

---

[25] *The Seven Habits of Highly Effective People*, Steven Covey, Simon & Schuster, New York, NY, 1989.

opportunity to collaborate and move forward often outweighs the cost. This is particularly true in matrix organisations where contexts and values are formed by functional cultures and people tend to persuade from and defend their functional viewpoint. They find it difficult to find a way of working together for a different end result.

In other situations, it may not be possible to reach a new end point, and it may not be necessary. The increased understanding engendered by the process may allow you to disagree harmoniously and respect your different positions more. After inquiry and advocacy on both sides, you disagree on the basis of understanding and empathising, not from a dogmatic perspective. This allows you to work together and not be antagonistic.

REFRAMING A DIFFICULT SITUATION

You can also have an impact on difficult situations by understanding more of your own thinking process – reflecting on the assumptions and beliefs that underpin your actions and correcting some which may be flawed in order to "reframe" the situation so you have a better chance of having a productive discussion. This is particularly effective if you continue to have a difficult relationship with the same person or group.

In situations of difficult conversations (people are resisting your proposals, you can't get agreement with close colleagues, you are being treated unfairly, someone else is not doing their job properly) Professor Argyris found that - *invariably* - the speaker defined themselves positively (I am right, I have the answer, I am being reasonable…) and the other person was seen negatively (she is wrong, he doesn't understand, she is not being reasonable, they have a hidden agenda.). It therefore follows that you will define your task in this "frame of reference" to persuade the other to see the error of their ways, prove them wrong. Indeed it is your duty to help them to see the error of their ways, and if they don't, it is their fault, not yours! And, not surprisingly, you get the outcome that you expected – an unproductive point/counterpoint discussion with both parties defending their "right" conclusion.

How can you break into this self-fulfilling prophecy?

You need first to understand your own thinking process. What are the assumptions you am making which could be guiding you into a negative position? A tool for this is to create a "Left Hand Column" dialogue:

First choose a difficult conversation, such as suggested earlier and remind yourself of the actual dialogue exchange. A good way to do this is to take a sheet of paper and divide it into two columns, and write the dialogue as you remember it in the right-hand column.

Then go back to the beginning and in the left-hand column write down the thoughts or feelings which were in your mind as you recalled yourself having that dialogue. What were you thinking and feeling when you were speaking? What were you thinking and feeling when you were listening to the other party?

CASE STUDY: A DIFFICULT TELEPHONE CONVERSATION

This conversation is between a sales agent and an account manager about a client proposal. First the dialogue as Samir, the sales agent, recalls it:

Samir: *Hi Karen, it's Samir here. Just wanted to check the position with ABC Company? The conversation I had with their MD suggested it was an urgent need.*

Karen: Hi Samir. Nothing yet. I left a message and I am waiting for them to return my call.

Samir: *The MD was really keen that we get something in place quickly. We have got a good opportunity here.*

Karen: I have put a call into their HR manager and I know she is very busy, I'm waiting for her to call me back.

Samir: *Why didn't you call the MD direct?*

Karen: I don't have a connection there. My contact is the HR manager. She makes all of the training decisions.

Samir: *But it was the MD who wanted this.*

Karen: I know, but I need to go through Claire. I don't have a direct contact with the MD...

Samir: (interrupting): *I do...*

Karen: (continuing): ...it wouldn't look right to go over her head to the MD.

Samir: *I don't think you need to be so careful. The HR manager will do whatever the MD tells her to.*

Karen: I don't want to upset Claire. They are big customers of ours.

Samir: *So when will you follow up?*

Karen: I'll try again on Monday.

Samir: *OK. Thanks. Bye.*

Then Samir's internal (unspoken) thoughts and feelings:

Thoughts and Feelings	Dialogue	
"What's the delay? I should have heard something by now." (FRUSTRATED)	Samir:	*Hi Karen, it's Samir here. Just wanted to check the position with ABC Company? The conversation I had with their MD suggested it was an urgent need.*
	Karen:	Hi Samir. Nothing yet. I left a message and I am waiting for them to return my call.
"That's not right. Has she done anything? I had better explain the urgency again... ...and the sales opportunity."	Samir:	*The MD was really keen that we get something in place quickly. We have got a good opportunity here.*
	Karen:	I have put a call into their HR manager and I know she is very busy, I'm waiting for her to call me back.
"Why HR? She's avoiding." (SUSPICIOUS)	Samir:	*Why didn't you call the MD direct?*
	Karen:	I don't have a connection there. My contact is the HR manager. She makes all of the training decisions.
"Excuses. Excuses. She just didn't want to do it."	Samir:	*But it was the MD who wanted this.*
	Karen:	I know, but I need to go through Claire. I don't have a direct contact with the MD...
"Tell her again..."	Samir:	(interrupting): *I do...*
	Karen:	(continuing): ...it wouldn't

		look right to go over her head to the MD.
"Same excuse. Avoiding again." (ANGRY)	Samir:	*I don't think you need to be so careful. The HR manager will do whatever the MD tells her to.*
	Karen:	I don't want to upset Claire. They are big customers of ours.
"I shouldn't need to tell her how to do her job!"	Samir:	*So when will you follow up?*
	Karen:	I'll try again on Monday.
"She is incompetent. Write this opportunity off. Silly *#!@#!!" (ANGER)	Samir:	*OK. Thanks. Bye.*

When Samir looks at his left hand column dialogue, he notices that he had probably started to create the outcome before he picked up the telephone! He was certainly not in a frame of mind to listen to what Karen was doing, or to see any of her actions in a positive light. His assumptions throughout are that he knows what she should have done; he would have done this better himself (although he does not offer to do so); she is incompetent, delaying, avoiding. All of the data in the phone call was filtered through these assumptions and reinforced them.

The "frame" Samir creates for Karen is that she is incompetent, lazy and avoids taking direct action. It is his duty to make her see that, accept she is in the wrong, and agree to do things his way.

But is Samir right? Is Karen incompetent, lazy and avoiding? Might it be that he is wrong – or at least partly wrong? Is he only seeing one side of the situation? Could it be that Karen is, in fact, good at her job, professional, very busy and sensitive to making and keeping good relationships with clients? Even if that is only partly true (and in Karen's case it is wholly true as an analysis of her success with account management proves), it allows Samir to enter the dialogue with a different set of assumptions and a different frame of reference – and then, probably get a different result. Samir could hear that she is busy and trying to follow up on the lead. He could recognise the relationship issue with Claire and offer to make contact with the MD himself – he has a direct link, so protects Karen's relationship with Claire. He could offer to help.

Viewing the data in a different light, with a different "frame", allows you to develop the potential for different outcomes.

This exercise is fairly easy when you reflect after the event. It allows you to think about the way in which you interact with some of your important connections where you are not getting the results you expect or need. It gives you the opportunity to prepare for the next conversation with a different frame. It is more difficult to notice, and react, when you are in the conversation – this needs practice.

DEVELOPMENT EXERCISES

1. WORDS, MUSIC AND DANCE

- Watch people in everyday situations to become more aware of Music and Dance people use.

- When you find yourself questioning what the other person is saying, reflect on what messages you are receiving from the Words, Music and Dance. Where is there an incongruity?

- Analyse your telephone conversations and emails – how easy is it to misunderstand the communication?

How can you improve your sending messages in these media to avoid miscommunication?

- Practise putting more emphasis and expression in your voice. Use some of the exercises that actors use to "warm-up":
  - o Record yourself and analyse the playback.
  - o Relax your body to clear tension from the muscles that will replay through the voice.
  - o Take slow, deep breaths. Breathe in to a count of 4 and out to a count of 7.
  - o Increase your breathing capacity – breathe from your diaphragm: Rest one hand on your stomach. As you breathe in, feel your stomach move outwards. As you breathe out, feel it moving inwards.
  - o Relax your facial muscles to enable you to enunciate words easily: Pull faces! Chew vigorously. Say some "tongue twisters" out loud.
  - o Stand with your chin up so that the voice is not constricted.
  - o Read through some simple passages of text – out loud – with different tempo and phrasing, emphasis and volume, in order to generate variety. Record yourself doing this and play back the recording. Experiment with going "over the top" to find your range.
- Use a video recorder to give yourself feedback on gestures and posture:
  - o Relax the body
  - o Deliver some different passages of text to camera with different gestures that emphasise the message in the text. Children's stories are good here, as are famous speeches from plays.

o Notice how the voice messages change when you use more emphatic gestures

o Again, experiment with "going over the top" to find your range and also to recognise that although you may feel uncomfortable when you are doing it, it is perfectly acceptable when you watch it!

2. INQUIRY AND ADVOCACY

- Practise with a friend or colleague. Take a subject on which you both have strong (and different) ideas. Suspend your thinking and **inquire** into your partner's thinking on the subject – do not defend your position – concentrate on getting to a level of understanding (empathy) with their position. Then **advocate** your position by explaining your reasoning, expressing your conclusion as an option, not a dogma, and helping your partner to understand you.

3. LEFT-HAND COLUMN

- Take a difficult conversation you have had and conduct a left-hand column exercise. Check your assumptions. Share your findings with a friend or colleague to get their insights. How can you reframe the situation to get a different result?

- Do a left-hand column exercise with a positive conversation you have had recently. What do you notice when you compare the thoughts and feelings in the left hand column with those from a difficult conversation? Can you transfer these thoughts and feelings (values) into other conversations?

PART TWO

DEVELOPING THE STYLES

CHAPTER SIX

OPTIMISING OPPORTUNITIES FOR GETTING RESULTS

"Words mean exactly what you want them to mean, no more and no less. It's all a question of showing them whose master, that's all."

LEWIS CARROLL

"There are really only three types of people: those who make things happen, those who watch things happen, and those who say, 'What happened?'"

ANN LANDERS

Part 1 explored the influencing arena from the perspectives of people's preferred styles of influence, how people communicate with each other and how emotional responses sometimes hijack our intent to deal with a situation in a positive way.

Part 2 further investigates the impact of the four influencing styles, and develops both breadth and depth of skill in the styles.

Breadth of skill so that you can flexibly use any of the four styles depending on the person you are trying to influence or the situation you face. Being able to speak the same "language" as the person you are trying to influence allows you to be understood. Using the style that gives you the best chance of reaching the outcome you want will enable you to get the desired results.

Developing depth of skill will give you the confidence to use any style through using the specific behaviours and actions that make up each style.

Each chapter looks at one of the styles in detail, following the same format, with some development exercises which you can use to practice and gain confidence and competence. Each style is equally important in achieving success in getting results with the range of people with whom you come in contact.

You may find that a good place to start is to look at the style you find least comfortable or use least, as identified in the questionnaire, rather than reading each chapter in sequence. Then look at the other styles in order of preference, finishing with your strongest preference – this style should be more familiar to you.

The first chapter is Action, followed by Process, People and finally Ideas.

EXPLORING THE FOUR INFLUENCING STYLES IN DEPTH

It is theoretically possible to use any influencing style in any situation and have a successful outcome. However, some situations lend themselves to a particular approach in order to either achieve the best outcome, or be most efficient. It is, for instance, possible to respond to an emergency situation by considering feelings and seeking everyone's understanding using People style to obtain a consensus, but it is clearly more appropriate to use Action style and get a quick response.

Each style has a different outcome when used in a situation. So, it is possible to analyse the situation and determine the desired outcome, and therefore choose the style that has the best chance of delivering that outcome. The behaviours and outcomes for each style are summarised on Figure 6-1.

There are situations that lend themselves to a particular style – like Action style being best in an emergency situation. For each of the styles there are tips on when to use the style so that you can identify where you might benefit from the use of that style.

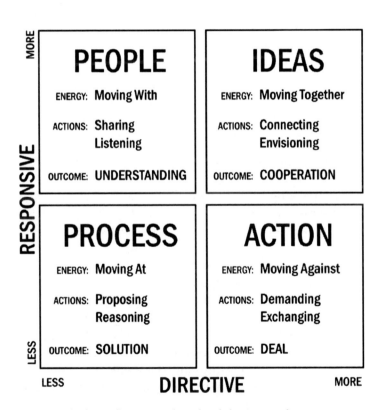

Figure 6-1: The four influencing styles – their behaviours and outcomes

There are specific behaviours associated with each style, which are emphasised by the congruent use of the Words, Music and Dance specific to that style. For all of the styles, the best and most effective impact comes from using both of the behaviours together. For example, in Action style, the potential aggressive demand is tempered and made acceptable by the exchange; in Ideas style, a great vision will only inspire someone if there is some common ground or connection to the other party. Ineffective use of the style is often related using only one of the behaviours, or getting them out of balance. For example, you can create a feeling of manipulation if you only listen to others' feelings and concerns and do not share your own; just making a proposal without any justification or supporting data is unlikely to be accepted. You need to practice getting the behaviours in balance in order to make the style effective. In each style section, there is a description of the behaviours, the Words, Music and Dance.

Finally, for each style, there are some ways to modify your natural speech patterns, so that you can adapt to communicating with someone who has a particular style preference. Without moving completely into a style in order to achieve a specific influence objective, it is possible to modify some elements of your own style so that the other person can hear you more clearly. You move closer to their way of speaking, matching the content, pace and tempo of their preferred style. This approach requires less preparation and involves less risk than trying to use a very unfamiliar style, with the dangers inherent in putting yourself under extra stress, but does have a positive impact on the relationship and the ability to understand each other as the other party recognises you are speaking the same "language."

CHAPTER SEVEN

ACTION STYLE

"Do or do not. There is no 'try'."
YODA

"There are risks and costs to a programme of action but they are far less than the long-range risks and costs of comfortable inaction."
JOHN F KENNEDY

MAKING EFFECTIVE DEALS BY BALANCING DEMANDS AND EXCHANGES

Action style is focused on getting results and moving on with a strong task focus. It is great for situations when there is little time to discuss options – if there is an emergency situation, you do not want to sit around discussing what it feels like to be in danger, using People style, you want someone to take action and get everyone to safety. Later, when there is time, some reflection and understanding on what caused the emergency and understanding personal reactions to it might be helpful, but not in the middle of the danger.

Underuse of this style means that you will not be able to get things done quickly and may miss deadlines. The people you work with may not have the clarity about what precisely you want from them and by when. Overuse and you could be perceived as arrogant and aggressive. An imbalance of the two actions, for instance, just demanding, especially if you do it a lot, is likely to give a dictatorial feel – only interested in getting what you want and not giving anything in return.

> *"I need the report by Friday."*

> *"I want you to go to the meeting this afternoon for me."*

By putting an exchange with the demand, the feeling is more of balance and fairness rather than imposition.

> *"I need the report by Friday, if you get it to me by then I will make sure that your manager knows that you are doing a great job on this project."*

> *"I want you to go to the meeting this afternoon for me, if you do, then I will attend the meeting for you next week."*

Effective use of the style comes from balancing both of the behaviours – Demanding and Exchanging. The outcome is a DEAL:

> *"If you agree to do X for me, I will do Y for you."*

> *"In return for the car, I will give you the money."*

Like all deals that are negotiated, they will only last as long as the deal is valid and they will typically deliver compliance with the terms of the deal. If that is acceptable to you, then Action style may be appropriate in that situation. If, however, you want someone's broader commitment, then the situation implies that Action style is not appropriate.

Action style depends on the exchange you can make to influence someone to do something for you. The exchange can be obvious and material, based on resource, position or information power: a tip, promotion, pay increase, gifts, and information that the other needs. Exchanges can also be less obvious and not material, based more on personal power: approval, status, attention, praise, inclusion, and time. These latter, psychological exchanges are often more powerful and longer lasting than material ones.

The exchange backs up the demand that you are making. It has to be something that you, as the giver, have to offer, something that the receiver desires, and something the receiver considers of sufficient value to balance the demand made. The critical point for the influencer is that it is the perception of value and balance in the eyes of the receiver which is important, not the giver's idea of what is appropriate. Thus something of low cost to the giver, like praise, can be viewed as of immense value by the receiver.

A positive exchange (an incentive) is always more effective than a negative exchange (usually perceived as a threat), and will have the effect of at least maintaining the relationship with the other party. If you want to add pressure and importance to the deal, then a combination of a positive and negative exchange will make the consequences of the deal clear:

> *"I need the report by Friday, if you get it to me by then I will make sure that your manager knows that you are doing a great job on this project. If you do not, then I will make sure your manager knows that you are hindering progress on this project."*

> *"I want to limit the discussion time in this meeting, if you agree, then I will make sure that we will finish early. If you don't, then I will not close the meeting until all of the agenda is covered."*

The exchange should be explicit. The implicit exchange is often assumed, and overestimated – thus a simple request for information (especially when the speaker has position power) becomes a threat of losing your job or an expectation of a reward which is not forthcoming. If you can't think of an exchange, but still want to use Action style, then ask the other person what they want in exchange:

> *"I need the report by Friday, what can I do for you in return?"*

> *"I want to limit the discussion time in this meeting, what do I need to do for you to agree to this?"*

So in summary:

WHEN TO USE ACTION STYLE:

- A deal is acceptable to both parties.

- There is little time to discuss.

- You both have something to exchange that the other wants.

- Compliance is acceptable to both parties.

- You have no logical reasons or the other's reasons for not agreeing are better than yours in support (you will therefore lose a rational discussion).

HOW TO USE ACTION STYLE:

Use both behaviours together.

DEMANDING

- Say exactly what you want
- Make forceful demands

EXCHANGING

- Offer to make a deal
- Offer something in return for what you want

Action style can be enhanced by considering the Words, Music and Dance associated with the style. Typical words that indicate Action style are: "I", "want", "demand", "need", "expect", "require", "offer", "deal", "exchange" , and "if you... then I". Action style is typified by "I" statements.

The music or tone of voice associated with Action style is authoritative, forceful, strong, clear, emphatic, punchy, abrupt, and blunt. It is not loud or shouting. The dance uses crisp and forceful gestures. Metaphorically (or actually) standing opposite people, point at them, looking at people in the face (to make it clear you are directing towards them, but without too much eye contact which may distract and influence you away from your objective). The posture is erect and rooted (something that is used by telephone callers when they want to sound more authoritative or say "no" – they stand up).

If you do not have an Action preference, then you will need to work on a number of changes to your preferred style to be able to speak the same language as someone with an Action preference. Choose your preferred style and follow the tips for success to adapt your natural style to sound more acceptable to an Action style person:

TO ADAPT TO ACTION

from Process...	from People...	from Ideas...
If your preference is for Process, then your focus on task and your objective approach (less responsive) will be appreciated. Your difference is on the directive scale, where you like to proceed at a more deliberate, low key pace.	If your preference is for People, then you differ in both the directive and responsive scales. You tend to do things slower and more deliberately; and you are more tuned into feelings whereas action people are focused on the task.	If you have an Ideas preference then you have some commonality with Action people in that you are both more directive than most; and your energy and fast pace will be appreciated. However, you are more responsive, which means you are willing to spend time on people issues rather than the task at hand.

So to adapt from Process to Action:

1 Pick up your pace.
Move and speak more quickly than usual. Address problems and make decisions quickly. Respond promptly.

2 Be energetic.
Maintain an erect posture, maintain eye contact and use emphatic gestures.

3 Focus on the big picture.
Concentrate on priority issues and avoid too much detail and theory.

So to adapt from People to Action:

1 Pick up your pace.
Move and speak quickly. Address problems and make decisions quickly. Respond promptly.

2 Be energetic.
Maintain an erect posture, maintain eye contact and use emphatic gestures.

3 Say what you think.
Action people want things done in a hurry. They are focused on goals and deadlines. Always keep commitments made to action people.

So to adapt from Ideas to Action:

1 Be more task oriented.
Be punctual and get right down to business. Tone down your speech and dress.

2 De-emphasise feelings.
Limit facial expressions and physical gestures. Avoid touch. Speak more forcefully. Say what you "think" not what you "feel".

4 *Focus on results.* Emphasise a pragmatic approach and focus on the results of the actions being discussed. 5 *Allow some freedom.* Don't impose unnecessary rules and procedures. Be clear about what you want, but allow them to set their objectives. 6 *Say what you think* Speak up more often and don't be afraid to disagree. Tell rather than ask.	4 *Be more task oriented.* Be punctual and get right down to business. 5 *De-emphasise feelings.* Keep to the point and use factual evidence, but don't go into detail. Limit your statements to the main points and focus on goals and results (especially if they involve a degree of stretch) rather than detail processes.	3 *Set clear goals and deliver them.* Action people aren't interested in dreams. Be realistic and plan your work. 4 *Be organised, factual and brief.* Be fully prepared. Focus on results and be pragmatic.

DEVELOPMENT EXERCISES

PRACTISING ACTION STYLE

- Find someone with whom to practise, and get feedback (ideally someone who has a preference for Action style as they can give you feedback on what is most effective for them).

- When you ask them to help you, use the Action style: Make a clear **demand** about what you want them to do. Tell the other person exactly what you will do for her or him in **exchange**.

- Role play different situations with them where you might need to use Action style in real life. E.g. ask them to take the role of someone from whom you need some information but who does not work directly for you. **Demand** from this person that she or he gives you the information you need. Tell them what you want and exactly what you will do for her or him in **exchange**. Ask them to take the role of your boss. **Demand** from your boss that she or he allows you to take full responsibility for a project. Offer an **exchange** in return.

- Get feedback from your partner on how you can improve your content and style, paying particular notice of the Words, Music and Dance.

CHAPTER EIGHT

PROCESS STYLE

"This paper by its very length defends itself against being read."
WINSTON CHURCHILL

"First learn the meaning of what you say, and then speak."
EPICTETUS

USING RATIONAL ARGUMENTS TO FIND LOGICAL SOLUTIONS

Process style uses logical reasoning and debate in order to create structure in data and facts, and by analysis find the best SOLUTION to the problem or situation being faced. It is less directive than Action style – those using Process style either do not have the answer (and cannot therefore be directive) or have the belief that their answer is just one option and is probably no better than anyone else's. So they wish to engage in debate and analysis to discover the best solution.

That means it will take longer to get to the outcome than with Action style. Overuse or an imbalance of the two actions in this style can lead to bureaucracy, long and boring meetings, and slavish following of procedures and rules – even when it is clear that the procedure is not effective. But it is a favourite style of many organisations as it allows some degree of participation in decision making and restricts the potential for abuse of power. It is not an appropriate style to use if there is a need for a quick decision, or where you are not open to other options.

Effective use of the style comes from balancing both of the behaviours – Proposing and Reasoning. The outcome is a SOLUTION:

> *"I propose that we complete the report by Friday. I have two reasons for this: firstly, it allows us to keep to the timetable that was agreed for the project; secondly, it gives us all time to gather and analyse the information needed."*

> *"The conclusion from the analysis of the data suggests that we take this course of action."*

> *"Weighing up the arguments on both sides, there is nothing to be gained from taking immediate action. The decision deadline is not until the end of the financial year, and there is no penalty for delaying the decision. Delaying the decision and gathering more data is the best solution."*

Proposals need to be clearly stated. It seems to be a trait, particularly of the British, that we are not precise in our proposals:

> *"I wonder whether it would be acceptable to the group to consider the possibility of completing the report by the end of the week, despite the difficulties that that may cause,"* does not have the same impact as *"I propose that we complete the report by Friday."*

In meetings and discussion, it is often easier to argue against a proposal than to suggest an alternative. In these situations, if you want to increase your influence in the use of Process style, ask for an alternative proposal. You can then discuss the merits of the alternatives in a positive environment, rather than find yourself in a defending role. You are open to rational response in Process style, but you still want to influence:

> *"I hear and understand your objections to my proposal; it would be good to hear your alternative proposal so that we can discuss what is best. If there is no alternative, then this proposal is the best option to doing nothing."*

The reasons backing up the proposal need to be valid and based on facts and logic. It is the weight of argument which influences, not in quantity but in quality. Reasoning that is geared towards the receiver, not the influencer, has the most impact. A strong reason for doing something from one perspective may hold no weight for the other person. So thinking in terms of benefits and what is important to the receiver is vital for success.

Quantity of argument is attractive, but ineffective, often seen as trying to wear down the other party into submission through the sheer weight of data and argument. Process style has a tendency toward the verbose, so you need to control the urge to continue speaking after the point is made. Then you don't find yourselves snatching defeat from the jaws of victory by having to defend a poorly researched piece of data or rationale which was not necessary in the first place.

With proper preparation, a good proposal should not need more than two or three reasons to back it up. As a good friend, colleague and mentor, Walt Hopkins puts it: *"Propose precisely, Reason concisely, then Shut up nicely."*

So in summary:

WHEN TO USE PROCESS STYLE:
- A solution is acceptable
- There is time to discuss
- You have good ideas
- You have good logical reasons and factual data
- You are open to rational response and debate

HOW TO USE PROCESS STYLE:

Use both behaviours together.

PROPOSING

- Propose solutions

- Make suggestions

REASONING

- Use facts and data to support my ideas

- Use logic and reasoning to argue against others suggestions

The Words, Music and Dance of Process are very different to those of Action style. Words you will hear and use to construct Process statements include "propose", "suggest", "think", "consider", "what if we tried to...", "my reasons are...", "reason", "logic", and "rationale". The tone of voice is calm, sensible, precise, articulate, even-paced and patterned – reflecting the structured and organised approach of the style. The dance is typified by looking away from people – the documents and data are more important than the people, so there is constant reference to and pointing at the data, the PowerPoint presentation, the budget numbers... People have a calm expression and use precise gestures, often counting points on fingers. It is the sort of environment when people can go to sleep! This often happens when Process style is ineffectually used.

Process style is so common in use in education and organisations that many people are comfortable using the style. However, it may not be your preferred style and so in order to adapt to be effective with someone who has a Process preference, you will need to make some adjustments from your preferred style:

TO ADAPT TO PROCESS

from Action...	from People...	from Ideas...
If you have an Action preference, you are similar in having a task focus, but you are more directive than a Process person. To adapt to Process from Action: *1 Slow your pace.* Move and speak more slowly than usual. Don't set tight deadlines. Don't rush their decisions. Take the time to be thorough. *2 Listen more and better.* Process people find it difficult to express themselves under pressure. Talk less and pause more often and for longer to give them openings.	With a People style preference, you share the less directive approach, so your low key style is appreciated. You differ on the responsiveness scale - you are more tuned into feelings whereas process people are focused on the task. To adapt to Process from People: *1 Be more task oriented.* Be punctual and get right down to business. *2 De-emphasise feelings.* Limit your facial expressions and physical gestures. Avoid touch (except for formalities). Speak directly. Say what you "think" not what you "feel." Use analytical words.	If you have an Ideas style preference, you need to adapt your style in both dimensions: you tend to do things quicker and more emphatically, and you are more tuned into feelings rather than the task. To adapt to Process from Ideas: *1 Slow your pace.* Move and speak more slowly than usual. Use more facts and data. Take the time to be thorough. *2 Listen more and better.* Talk less and pause more often and for longer to give them openings. *3 Don't come on too strong.* Process people like time to consider things and need time to express themselves effectively. So talk less and slower and don't rush their decisions. Tone

3 *Don't come on too strong.* Decrease eye contact, reduce gestures and lean back. Ask rather than tell, for example "Here's an idea..." rather than "This is what to do..."	3 *Have a detailed plan.* Process people like to work to detailed plans and procedures. Plan your work and work your plan. 4 *Be detailed and factual.* Well organised, factual evidence (and the more detail the better) will influence Process people more than slick presentation.	down the music so as not to appear too emotional. 4 *Be more task oriented.* Be punctual and get down to business. Keep to the point. 5 *De-emphasise feelings.* You like spontaneity and improvisation, whereas process people like detailed, structured plans. So be well organised and use factual evidence, with as much detail as possible.

DEVELOPMENT EXERCISES

PRACTISING PROCESS STYLE

- Find someone with whom to practise, and get feedback (ideally someone who has a preference for Process style as they can give you feedback on what is most effective for them).

- Make a **proposal** to your partner that they do something to improve their health (stop smoking, take more exercise, etc. – ideally something that they want to do). Support your proposal with data and logical **reasoning** (and try to structure your reasoning to focus on what is important to the other person rather than just good data).

- **Propose** that your partner work with you on an activity. Use no more than two **reasons** to justify your proposal. The other person can resist if the reasoning is not sound.

- Role play some situations that are real or difficult for you. E.g. ask your partner to take the role of your boss. **Propose** that she or he allows you to attend a three week training course in the USA. Use no more than three **reasons** in support.

- Get feedback from your partner on how you can improve your content and style, paying particular notice of the Words, Music and Dance.

PROCESS STYLE

CHAPTER NINE

PEOPLE STYLE

"A good listener is not only popular everywhere, but after a while he gets to know something."
WILSON MIZNER

"Seek first to understand, then to be understood."
STEVEN COVEY

LISTENING EMPATHETICALLY TO GENERATE UNDERSTANDING

People style is the only style that gathers information, so it is very useful to help find out what values and desires the other party has which can then be used as possible exchanges, reasons or connections. It therefore has a strong strategic use. It also builds relationships with others through developing deeper understanding of each other. It is therefore a key style to use where relationship and trust are critical.

People style is the key to effective coaching – using questioning and listening skills to help someone to solve a problem for themselves and develop their abilities. In this sense it is also a positive form of influence in its own right. You can get people to do things and build a relationship simultaneously.

But it does take much more time than any of the other styles, both to build the rapport and to listen effectively to check your understanding about what was said and to probe for deeper insight into the thinking of the other person. However, if it is important to have a clear understanding of the underlying needs of your manager, your customer, project sponsor or colleague, then it is time and effort that is well spent.

Like all other styles, overuse or over dependence on one style will mean that you have difficulty interacting with others who have a different preference. At least the characteristic sensitivity of People style should enable you to identify such a difficulty quickly, and do something about it.

Effective use of People style, as with all of the other styles, comes from balancing both of the behaviours – Sharing and Listening. The outcome is UNDERSTANDING:

> *"I am confused by the aims of this project and I need your help to understand what I need to focus on (Sharing)... If I hear you correctly, your priority is that we must keep to the time deadlines at all costs. Could you expand on the importance of keeping to time so I can understand why it is more important than keeping to the specification? (Listening)"*

Sharing allows me to open up to the other party and show that you are willing to disclose information and feelings that are usually private. This builds trust and gives the other party the confidence to reciprocate – to tell you the depth of information you need to fully understand. Sharing too much will tend to have the opposite effect and erode trust as people will feel "dumped" upon. Listening too much will also raise mistrust and the feeling of being manipulated, so it is important to balance sharing with listening.

Empathetic listening is listening with the intent to understand. It is the highest level of listening and the others being:

- Ignoring (arguably not listening at all, just hearing): staying quiet but not paying any attention to what the person is saying;
- Pretending: Using verbal or non-verbal clues but not really listening;
- Selective: hearing only certain parts of what the person is saying – usually those parts we agree with; and
- Attentive: actively paying attention and focusing on understanding what is being said.

Empathetic listening is listening to really understand the other person's frame of reference – to see and feel the world as they do[26].

This level of listening allows you to carry out the sort of inquiry process that was discussed in the last chapter – helping people down the Ladder of Inference so that you can create a greater appreciation of the data sources and thinking processes that bring the other person to their conclusion. It helps you to understand, and it also fosters understanding in the other party.

Some tips for listening empathetically:

> *Be Quiet*
> That means to stop talking to yourself in your head (e.g. rehearsing your next question) as well. If the other person stops talking, count to three before saying anything. If they continue talking, keep quiet.

---

[26] *The Seven Habits of Highly Effective People*, Steven Covey, Simon & Schuster, New York, NY, 1989.

Be attentive

Focus all your attention on the other person. Use your own music and dance to let the other person know that you are paying attention.

Suspend Judgement

Clear your mind of your own thoughts. Do not make judgements based on your own views or perceptions. Seek to understand the other person's views and perceptions before expressing your own.

Understanding is not necessarily agreeing

The objective is to understand, not to agree. You don't need to defend your ideas or position in order to understand the other's.

Paraphrase and summarise frequently

Summarise the message in your own words. CHECK with the other person that you have got the right message. Do this more frequently than you think is necessary – it demonstrates your interest and understanding. Always paraphrase before asking a question – it should flow naturally; if not don't ask the question!

Listen to Feelings

Share your own feelings. Pay attention to the signals (verbal and non-verbal) that indicate what the other person might be feeling. Summarise these and CHECK to see if you have guessed correctly.

Encourage Possibilities

Use open questions to encourage the other person to consider other possibilities. Do NOT give advice or state your own opinions.

So in summary:

WHEN TO USE PEOPLE STYLE:
- Generating understanding is the ideal outcome
- There is time to engage in empathetic listening
- You need commitment
- There are strong feelings present
- You are willing to share your feelings

HOW TO USE PEOPLE STYLE:
Use both behaviours together.

SHARING
- Share your feelings
- Disclose information

LISTENING
- Check to establish understanding
- Encourage deeper sharing around feelings, beliefs and values

The Words, Music and Dance of People are unique to the style. Words you will hear include "I feel", "I'm concerned about", "I'm feeling", "I'm delighted about", "So you are saying...", "So far I have heard you saying...", and "Have I heard you correctly?" The tone of voice is attentive, concerned, relaxed, friendly, empathetic, tentative, slow, and pleasant – reflecting the style's need to establish an environment where it is easy to share information and take some risks. The dance is to sit with people (usually alongside, not in a confronting position), an open and attentive expression, eye contact is essential, and gestures tend to be tentative and encouraging.

If you are coming from a different preference than People and wish to communicate with someone who has a strong People preference, then you need to adjust your approach.

TO ADAPT TO PEOPLE

from Action...	from Process...	from Ideas...
If you have an Action preference, then you need to adapt your style in two ways: you differ on the directive scale, so People style people are uncomfortable with your pace and decisiveness. You are less responsive, which means you tend to be more aloof and task oriented.	From a Process preference, you have a less directive approach in common; and your slower pace is therefore appreciated. However, you are less responsive, which means you tend to be more task oriented and unemotional.	If you have an Ideas preference then you are both more responsive than most, so your warmth, friendliness and focus on people will be noticed. But you differ on the directive scale, so People style people are uncomfortable with your fast pace.
To adapt from Action to People:	To adapt from Process to People:	To adapt from Ideas to People:
1 *Make personal contact.* Be more casual and informal than usual. Talk about yourself and any other non-task related topic.	1 *Take the time to make personal contact.* Try to be more casual and informal than usual. Talk about yourself and any other non-task related topic.	1 *Slow your pace.* Talk slower. Don't set tight deadlines. Don't rush their decisions.
2 *Focus more on feelings.* People style people are supportive, and they expect others to be supportive. Listen empathetically so that they feel heard and understood. Show loyalty to others.	2 *Focus more on feelings.* People style people are more sensitive to the feelings of others and expect the same. But they are less talkative, so pay close attention to their dance.	2 *Listen more and better.* You tend to speak your mind. People style people are more likely to keep their opinions to themselves. So talk less and pause longer to give them openings.

3 *Slow your pace* Talk slower. Don't rush them. Don't force decisions. 4 *Listen more and better.* Talk less and pause longer to give them openings. Show you are listening by summarising. 5 *Don't come on too strong.* People style people do not like heavy-handed authoritarians. But they do appreciate stable, clearly structured situations. Make sure you establish clearly defined goals and jobs. Help them plan their work.	3 *Be supportive .* Listen effectively so they feel heard and understood. 4 *Show an interest in the human side.* Discuss the effects of decisions on people and invite their input. 5 *Limit facts and logic.* People style people are logical, but don't bury them under a pile of facts.	3 *Be supportive.* Listen empathetically so they feel heard and understood. Offer help. 4 *Don't come on too strong.* Decrease gestures and lean back, not forward. Tone down the music - People style people are softer spoken, you are the loudest speaker of all the styles.

DEVELOPMENT EXERCISES

PRACTISING PEOPLE STYLE

- Find someone with whom to practise, and get feedback (ideally someone who has a preference for People style as they can give you feedback on what is most effective for them).

- Practise **sharing** with your partner; take a range of topics with different disclosure risks and expand your "comfort zone" of disclosure:

  - o A work experience where you have felt really energised and successful;
  - o What makes you most proud;
  - o What makes you most afraid;
  - o Your heroes and heroines;
  - o A difficult situation that you have faced;
  - o Your dreams;
  - o Your fears; and
  - o "Advocate" your views on a controversial topic using the approach outlined in Chapter 5.

- Practise **listening** by getting your partner to share with you using the same topics. "Inquire" into your partner's views on a controversial topic using the approach outlined in Chapter 5.

- Get feedback from your partner on how you can improve your content and style, paying particular notice of the Words, Music and Dance.

CHAPTER TEN

IDEAS STYLE

"Leadership is the ability to align strengths toward a goal or vision in such a way that weaknesses are irrelevant."

PETER DRUCKER

"If the image means something to you, you can make it mean something to someone else. If it doesn't mean something to you, it can come across as fake and then you will be worse off than before."

RICHARD OLIVIER

BUILDING COOPERATION THROUGH VISIONS BASED ON VALUE CONNECTIONS

The Ideas style combines high responsive with high directive, it bases its influence on building strong connections with people and then directing that latent energy into a direction – a vision – that is the influencer's. It relies on generating enthusiasm and attracting people with some common ground to a common vision of what might be. In that sense it is quite idealistic, so the more far-sighted the vision, the deeper the connection has to be with the other party(ies) to make sure that they come with you. It is not worth having a great vision if people are not attracted to it and do not "buy in". Equally, having a great connection with people is a wasted opportunity if that energy is not channelled into a positive direction.

This is a style that is used (and misused) by political and business leaders worldwide. Look back at historical events in the growth of nations and organisations, and you often find a clear vision of the future being portrayed to an audience that has a high level of connectivity and common ground with the speaker (leader). In recent history, two examples are often quoted: the Rev. Martin Luther King "I have a dream..." speech and President John F Kennedy's "Man on the moon" speech. In the latter, Kennedy to the feelings and beliefs in the USA connected to the 1960s Cold War and the space race with very few words: *"I believe this nation should commit itself, to achieving the goal, before this decade is out, of landing a man on the moon and returning him safely to the earth,"* created the spark that led to major technological developments that allowed Neil Armstrong to take the first steps on the moon before the end of the decade (as envisioned).

What made this vision so powerful was the ability of people to visualise the success at the time of the speech in 1961 – ordinary people, and the technologists and scientists involved were able to immediately picture the image of a space-suited astronaut standing on the moon with an American flag. Once the image had been seen – albeit in the mind's eye – it is real, therefore it has happened and you can now stand in the future and look back to the present day and work out how you got here, knowing you have been successful. Standing in the present day and trying to push people towards the future causes resistance. Standing in the future and attracting people to you overcomes resistance.

Ideas style is also open to misuse, most obviously by dictators, cult leaders, politicians and some sales people. Just like any other style, the intent behind the use of the style needs to be positive otherwise it is manipulative. However, used effectively, it has the power to influence large groups of people and generate enthusiasm and team spirit, often overcoming barriers and rational objections.

It is a style of particular use in introducing change, as it is the power of the future possibilities which enables you to overcome the fear of taking the first step, just like the vision of the sunny beach on holiday helps overcome a fear of flying.

Ineffective leaders (at any level in an organisation) often have the vision of what they want to achieve, but do not have the responsiveness in their behaviour to build connections with their people. The vision therefore becomes an empty image, not relating to the reality or emotions of the staff, and not motivating them to change. Ordinary workers do not get excited about a corporate vision *"to increase shareholder value"* – it may work for the directors (who are also shareholders) but not for the rest.

The effective use of this style means taking time to connect with the values and beliefs of the whole group, and building exciting and attractive futures based on common ground.

> *"We all want to make the best product we can, we have all worked on highly successful product development in the past. Together we make a formidable team which I believe has the capability to produce the most successful product innovation in this Company's history. The ideas we have now are revolutionary. They will stun the world. We have the ability to put them into action. I can see us collecting awards from the industry at the technology forum next year. We are all there, proud of the results and amazed that we have managed to achieve so much in such a short space of time."*

Ideas style, in common with People style, builds commitment. Most of all it builds COOPERATION.

In summary:

WHEN TO USE IDEAS STYLE:

- You want to build cooperation;
- There is time to connect with the other person (not to find out *what* you have in common, but to articulate the connection and invest time in maintaining it. If you need to find out what common ground you might have, then you need to use People style first);
- You need commitment;
- You have ideas, beliefs and values in common; and
- You can envision exciting possibilities.

HOW TO USE IDEAS STYLE:

Use both behaviours together.

CONNECTING

- Establishing and stating what we both believe in
- Emphasise what we have in common

ENVISIONING

- Talking about what we can do together
- Focusing on future possibilities

The Words, Music and Dance of Ideas reflect the purpose and outcome of the style – idealistic, enthusiastic and inviting. The words include "we", "together", "team", "values", "achieve", "imagine", "vision", "mission", "goal", "future", and "possibilities". The tone of voice, or music is enthusiastic, intense, excited, committed, and varied. The dance is enthusiastic and uses dramatic gestures. The energy of moving together with the other party leads you to stand beside them, to reach out to connect and, look together towards a shared goal or imagined possibility.

If you are coming from a different preference than Ideas and wish to communicate with someone who has a strong Ideas preference, then you need to adjust your approach.

TO ADAPT TO IDEAS STYLE

from Action...	from Process...	from People...

Your energy and fast pace (more directive than most people) is something you have in common. But you differ on the responsiveness scale, so you tend to see friendly, informal contact as a waste of valuable time.
 	
To adapt from Action to Ideas:
 	
1 *Take more time to make personal contact.*
  Try to be more casual and informal than usual. Talk about non-task topics.
 	
2 *Focus more on feelings.*
  Acknowledge the expression of feelings from the Ideas person. Don't overreact to large mood swings or to verbal attack - Ideas people often exaggerate.
	Process style differs from Ideas style in both dimensions, so you need to show more warmth and friendly, informal contact, and raise your energy and pace.
	
	To adapt from Process to Ideas:
	
	1 *Make personal contact.*
	  Be more casual and informal. Talk about values and things you have in common.
	
	2 *Focus more on feelings.*
	  Ideas people are more responsive than you, so allow time to make connections and be prepared to talk about your feelings as well as the facts of a situation.
	
	3 *Pick up the pace.*
	  Move and speak more quickly than usual.
		From a People preference, you have a common dimension in being more responsive than most; your warmth and friendliness, and your people focus will be appreciated. However, as you are less directive, you tend to do things slower and more deliberately.
		
		To adapt from People to Ideas:
		
		1 *Pick up the pace.*
		  Move and speak more quickly than usual. Address problems quickly and be prepared to make quick decisions.
		
		2 *Be energetic.*
		  Use emphatic gestures and maintain an erect posture.

3 *Allow them more time.* Ideas people spend a lot of time thinking out loud. Give them some freedom here, even though it appears to be time-wasting. 4 *Give recognition and freedom.* Ideas people like an easy going, fun atmosphere to give of their best.	4 *Be more energetic.* Use enthusiastic gestures and move more. 5 *Say what you think.* Ideas people like spontaneity and improvisation, not detailed, structured plans. So give them freedom to try out new things and don't kill their ideas and dreams with too much realism. Limit rules and procedures. Don't overdo facts and logic.	3 *Focus on the big picture.* Concentrate on high priority issues with a broad brush approach. Avoid detail. 4 *Say what you think.* Speak up and don't be afraid to disagree. Tell rather than ask, for example "Here's what I think..." rather than "Do you think it makes sense to..."

DEVELOPMENT EXERCISES

PRACTISING IDEAS STYLE

- Find someone with whom to practise, and get feedback (ideally someone who has a preference for Ideas style as they can give you feedback on what is most effective for them).

- If you know your partner well, share what you see as ideas, experiences, values and beliefs you have in common to establish a **connection.** When you feel connected, try to use that connected energy to imagine achieving something together **(envision).** Encourage your partner to join in the vision and build on your images and visions. See how far you can take the vision before the connection is lost.

- Experiment with **envisioning** possibilities and positive outcomes with project teams or social/sport teams that you work with. Articulate what you see as the **connection** that binds you together and share your **vision**.

- Get feedback from your partner on how you can improve your content and style, paying particular notice of the Words, Music and Dance.

IDEAS STYLE

PART 3

APPLICATION

CHAPTER ELEVEN

PLANNING FOR SUCCESS

"We have a plan, therefore nothing can go wrong."
SPIKE MILLIGAN

"If you are leaping a ravine, the moment of take-off is a bad time to be considering alternative strategies."
JOHN CLEESE

This chapter puts all of the learning so far into the context of real life situations. What do you actually do in order to get better results from the situations you face? How can you give yourself the best chance of success in getting what you want and also build a better relationship with the other party?

There is a five step planning process and a planning guide for you to use in analysing and preparing for critical influence situations, and a couple of case studies which highlight the use of some of the tools available to you.

TACTICAL PLANNING

In a lot of situations, you can make an enormous difference to the relationship with the other party and to your ability to get results by just changing some of the tactical influence you use. You don't need to radically change your style, you just need to talk the same language as the person you are trying to influence.

Just like the archetypal Englishman abroad who discovers people don't suddenly understand English just because you speak it slower and louder, so people will respond better if you speak their style "language" rather than impose your different "foreign" style language on them. If you know a colleague has a preference for Action style, then use the principles of that style when you speak to them, and they will understand better what it is you want.

CASE STUDY: GETTING THE DESIRED RESULT FROM A MANAGER

Malcolm worked in a multi-national oil company, Process style was predominant, and was a particular preference of one of his line managers. After several disagreements and unsuccessful attempts to influence with his scrappy notes, ill-formed and conceptual ideas (from his Ideas style preference), Malcolm suddenly had a blinding flash of the obvious and presented his thoughts in detailed, systematic reports backed by analysis and data.

When he switched to using Process style, Malcolm's ideas were quickly accepted (often without the detail of the report and data being read fully) and he got the result he wanted. When Malcolm used one of his preferred styles, he did not get what he wanted, and at the same time he was worsening the relationship with his manager. It was not easy for him to put his ideas into written reports, collect the research data and develop the spreadsheets – but it was worth it to get the result he wanted.

So the first consideration in analysing and planning for situations is to become more aware of the preferences of your key influence targets, and know what you need to do to adapt your normal approach to meet the language expectations of the target. Make it easy for them to understand you, not difficult for them. You don't have to be word-perfect in their language, they will notice and appreciate the effort you are making and respond positively.

STRATEGIC PLANNING

On other occasions, a more strategic approach is needed. The situation may be complex, or there is a specific long-term outcome that is required. As covered in Part 2, each style gives a different outcome. So if you know the long term outcome you want this will guide your decision to the style that will give you the best chance of success. But it may not be possible to just use that style straight away and get a positive result. If, for instance, the chosen style is not the preference of the target, then there would be resistance – you would be talking a different language to the target. In these cases you would need to think of a strategic plan to get to the end outcome you want.

A FIVE STEP PLAN TO GETTING RESULTS

There is a Five-Step process for developing a plan, shown in Figure 11-1 below.

A FIVE-STEP PLAN FOR GETTING RESULTS

STEP 1: Who is Who?

STEP 2: Who am I? Who are you?

STEP 3: What do I want? What do you want?

STEP 4: Which style will give the greatest chance of success?

STEP 5: How do I get it?

Figure 11-1: A Five-Step strategic planning process

Looking at the five steps in detail:

STEP 1: WHO IS WHO?

The first question to resolve is: who is your target? In some situations this is easy – you have one person in mind who you need to influence: someone who needs to supply data to the project; a colleague who you want to invite to give their opinion on a report; a manager whose authority you need to proceed. If you can identify the two parties, then you can move directly to Step 2.

In other, more complex situations, the immediate target is not so easy to define. If the situation involves many people and/or is focused on a long-term goal or more general business objective, you first need to do some analysis to identify the priorities, and work out who to target first.

If you analyse a particular situation where you need to influence, there are probably a number of interested parties who have influence over the situation and have an interest in the outcome – STAKEHOLDERS. You may need to positively influence some or all these people in order to gain success in your overall aim.

There might also be other people whom you need to influence to achieve your aim – you need to be aware of the ORGANISATIONAL POLITICS and gain support for your main objective by influencing people who can help you, deal with their possible objections, help you to gain access to decision makers, and form alliances.

You can draw a map of the political or stakeholder environment, as in Figure 11-2, which will help you to analyse the situation and make some decisions about whom you need to influence:

- On a piece of paper in landscape form, draw a small circle in the centre containing the word ME.

- Add more circles for the different people, placing them near to or further away from the ME circle depending on the **strength of relationship** between you – the closer the circle, the stronger the relationship. Use the size of the circle to denote the **influence** of the person on the situation – the bigger the circle, the stronger and more important the influence.

- Finally draw a line between each new circle and the ME circle, using the thickness of line to show how **frequent** the interaction is between you and that stakeholder.

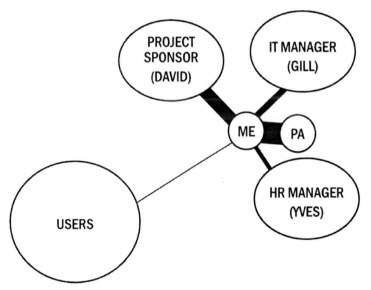

Figure 11-2: A Stakeholder map

The case of Mark, a project manager in an IT company, illustrates the use of Stakeholder Mapping:

CASE STUDY: MARK'S PROJECT

Mark's project is to improve the IT systems and processes so that they support the faster development of new products. He gets a quick briefing on the context and a rough scope from a senior manager sponsor, but there is a lot of ambiguity about precisely what is required.

The project sponsor is always very busy and is renowned for expecting people to "read between the lines" and understand her expectations. She has a strong preference for the Action style. Mark sees that in order to get the outcome he wants, he needs to use People style. He needs time to sit with the senior manager and ask a lot of questions in order to develop an understanding of the needs for this project; to get behind the headlines. He knows he could not just book an hour in her schedule – she never blocks that amount of time. So he decides to approach her in her preferred style, Action, to do a deal where the senior manager would commit to give some more time to him to explain the needs, and in return he gives a guarantee to deliver the project on time and on budget. The deal is acceptable, and Mark gets an extended time in the senior manager's agenda to engage in some People style sharing and listening. He clarifies the project deliverables and gets a detailed understanding of the priorities and needs of his sponsor.

He has overcome the first hurdle, now he sets down to some more detailed thinking about his influencing strategy for the project as a whole. Mark needs to identify all of the people who have an interest in the project – the stakeholders – and identify what their interests are, to develop a plan to deliver the results they want.

He also needs to think about the political environment in which he is operating – who does he need to influence in order to make sure that the project is successful? Where are his adversaries and allies? Who wants this project to succeed and who wants to see it fail? How can he deal with the politics so that he has the best chance of success (and deliver on his promised guarantee).

He sets about devising a strategic influence plan:

Mark has already identified that he needs to do some analysis of stakeholders and the politics of the situation. Starting at Step 1 – Who is who? He draws a stakeholder map (Figure 11-3):

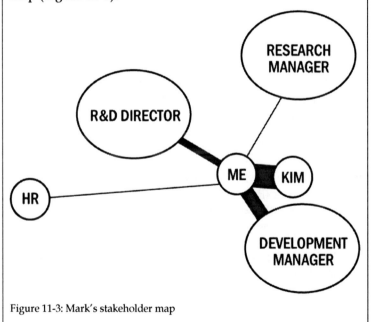

Figure 11-3: Mark's stakeholder map

Mark looked at this map and immediately got a clear picture of his priorities and needs:

- The three most important stakeholders are the R&D Director, the Research Manager and the Development Manager. Of the three, Mark had the weakest relationship with the Research Manager. He needed to spend some time here to build the relationship. Then he needed to strengthen the relationship with the R&D Director. His relationship with the Development Manager was better, and he met with him more frequently.

- Like all managers, Mark was already busy and had little time for more meetings. How would he find the time to devote to relationship building meetings with the Research Manager and the R&D Director? Looking at the map, he saw he had a very good relationship and a lot of meetings with Kim, his deputy. She was not influential or important in this project. So he could afford to delegate more responsibility on other operational issues to her in the short-term, have fewer meetings, and therefore free up time for his other priorities.

- He did not need to worry about HR in this project. They have little influence so his poor relationship and lack of contact was not important.

So Mark had identified his priorities and could now move on to Step 2 and complete a plan: first for Kim, then for the others.

STAKEHOLDER ANALYSIS[27]

At another level of detail in Step 1, you can conduct a STAKEHOLDER ANALYSIS to see where your stakeholders fit in terms of agreement with your intent and in terms of how much you trust them, as shown in Figure 11-4. This is particularly relevant for analysing the political dimensions at work in your scenario.

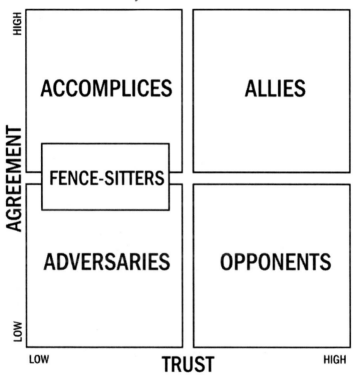

Figure 11-4: Stakeholder Analysis

---

[27] This model is from *The Empowered Manager* by Peter Block, Josey-Bass, San Francisco, 1988 p 132. Reproduced with permission.

Allies are those who are in agreement with your intent or project direction, and those you can trust, so you know that they will support and advocate for you. You can develop strategies to use your allies to help you to influence others.

Opponents are those who you know are against your proposal or project, but as you trust them, you know what their arguments are and that they will "fight fair". You can put together logical arguments to deal with their objections and hope to win them round. Or, you can enter into an open discussion to understand their concerns and build possible consensus and convert them to Allies.

Accomplices are those who appear to be in agreement with you, but as you have low trust with them, you cannot be 100% sure that when it comes to the final reckoning that they will support you. You need to build the relationship and therefore trust with them, so that you can identify whether or not they are truly in favour. You may find that your questioning their trust was misplaced, and that they move directly into the Allies box. Even if you find that they are against your idea, it is better to have them as a trusted Opponent than as an Accomplice. If your influence need is critical, you cannot afford to have any "question marks" around what might happen. You need to take positive steps to ensure the maximum chance of success. You need to be able to isolate or convert Accomplices, Adversaries and Fence-Sitters.

Adversaries are those with whom you are not in agreement and whom you do not trust. Again, you could try to build the relationship with them to make them into Opponents, and thus reduce the uncertainty over tactics. If they are particularly powerful, then this could be the best strategy. If there are few, not powerful adversaries, a less difficult strategy would be to find ways to isolate their impact, possibly by using your Allies to build protection. If there are a large number of people who fall into the Adversary camp, you may need to follow a very different influence strategy – abort the project and influence the sponsor that success is too difficult or not achievable.

Fence-Sitters are by definition ones who will not commit. They are automatically low trust, as if you had high trust; you would know where they sit. The strategy here mirrors that for Adversaries and Accomplices – you need to build trust so that you can discover in which of the four boxes they sit, and then take further action from there.

A further case study, that of Anne-Marie, an Account Manager in a technology application company, describe the use of the stakeholder analysis tool.

CASE STUDY: ANNE-MARIE'S KEY ACCOUNT PLANNING

Anne-Marie manages 3 key accounts, and in one of these her company is bidding to develop a new technology. This would be a significant contract, so she wants to ensure the best chance of success.

Starting at Step 1 – Who is who? She maps the stakeholders in the customer organisation who will have an impact on the decision to award the contract. Some of the stakeholders she knows well, others only by reputation, so she developed the analysis by talking to others in the account team and those who have dealings with this customer. She used the Stakeholder Analysis tool to summarise the thinking of the team (Figure 11-5):

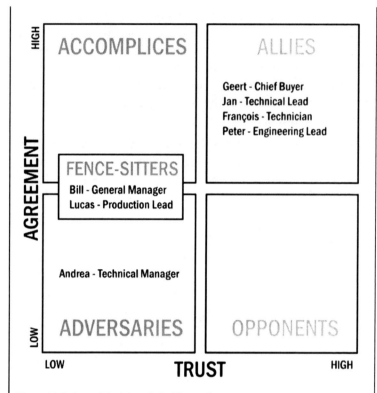

Figure 11-5: Anne-Marie's stakeholder analysis

Anne-Marie's first reaction was positive – her analysis and that of her colleagues put most of the key decision makers in the Allies box. Her company had a great relationship with the technical and engineering group in the customer for whom this technology was destined. She knew that they wanted to award the contract to her. She also had a strong relationship with Geert, the Dutch chief buyer for the group, and he had always expressed his preference for her organisation over their competitors.

However, she was concerned about the other three key decision influencers. In particular Andrea had only recently taken over as the Technical Manager in the customer's company. She had previously held a senior position in one of Anne-Marie's competitors, and this competitor was also bidding for this contract. Andrea had been the key technical lead for the competitor in this specialist product area. She was a real threat as she could favour her previous company, and no-one in the team had an established relationship with her. If anything, the relationship had been one of mistrust and competition when she was in the rival organisation.

There was also an issue with the General Manager and the Production Lead. Both of these would have an influence on the final decision, but there was absolutely no knowledge about their thinking or any real knowledge of them as individuals. They were Fence-Sitters precisely because Anne-Marie and their colleagues could not place them anywhere else.

Looking at this analysis, Anne-Marie devised a strategic influence plan with her colleagues that would give them the best chance of success. Their first priority had to be to build a better relationship with Andrea. A lot of their thinking about her was based on reputation and expectations that she would favour her previous employer. They needed to check these assumptions and build trust. It would be far better to know that she was in opposition to awarding the contract to Anne-Marie, and to know what the objections were.

It would be good to think that it was possible to turn Andrea into an Ally, but an Opponent is better than an Adversary. In the discussion, Anne-Marie and her colleagues also considered an alternative strategy to deal with an Adversary – isolation – find a way of limiting her impact on the decision. However, it was thought that Andrea's position as Technical Manager was too influential and powerful for this to be successful. Building a relationship and trust was the best option.

Next, the team considered the two Fence-Sitters and followed through their planning. When it came to Bill, the General Manager and Lucas, the Production Lead, no-one in Anne-Marie's team knew them or had a possibility to make a direct contact. These were second priorities to Andrea, but they could still continue to Step 2 in the planning process and work out how they would address each person in turn.

The outcome of Step 1 in the process is to identify the specific influence target that needs to be addressed first. Whether this has been easy – you already have someone in mind, or more complex, where you need to use the analysis tools, the result will be two parties that are identified: you and your target.

STEP 2: WHO AM I? WHO ARE YOU?

Having identified the two parties in the influence situation – you and your influence target, you can start to define in a little more detail your own thoughts and feelings as they apply to this situation and your role in it, and your thoughts and feelings about the target. Think of anything that may have an impact on the assumptions and frame of reference that you create for the situation. Your analysis may be different for the same person in different situations – the role you each play can change. You may be closer and more in agreement in some situations than in others. So it is important to identify the specific thoughts and feelings with the situation in mind, and not rely on previous experiences.

Then do the same for the other person. Use your knowledge of the other person to make the best decision you can – and also note where you have gaps in knowledge that stop you being able to make a judgement.

These are significant in helping you to choose an initial influence strategy – too many gaps about the other person suggest that you need to increase your understanding (using People style) so that you can then do a complete and better plan.

You can summarise your thinking on a Planning Guide, as shown in Figure 11-6:

WHO AM I? Name:	WHO ARE YOU? Name:	
Describe the situation and your role in it. What is your preferred style? What are your feelings and thoughts about the person who is the target of your influence?	*Put yourself in the position of the other person. Describe the situation and their role in it. What is their preferred style? What are their feelings and thoughts about you?*	
WHAT DO I WANT?	**WHAT DO YOU WANT?**	
List all of the things you would like to get from this situation. Circle the most important ones.	*Again from the perspective of the other person, list all of the things the other person might want. Circle the most important ones.*	
WHAT STYLE WILL GIVE ME THE BEST CHANCE OF SUCCESS?		
WHAT OUTCOME?	**OTHER'S STRENGTH?**	**IMPACT OF EACH**
What outcome do I want? Deal, Solution, Understanding, Cooperation.	*What is the strength of preference of the other party?*	*What would be the impact of each one of the styles?*
HOW DO I DO IT?		
What do I say in the chosen style? What words, music and dance fit? What about the physical environment? Where might difficulties occur? How will I respond to them? What do I need to practise?		

Figure 11-6: Planning Guide

STEP 3: WHAT DO I WANT? WHAT DO YOU WANT?

Next think about what it is that you want from the situation and what the other party might want.

What are the priorities of these wants? If you try to influence on too many fronts, try to pursue too many objectives at the same time, you may well confuse yourself and the other person and not achieve your main goal.

What is your main objective for THIS immediate situation?

Is there a sequence of influence objectives to get the eventual result that you are seeking? For example, if you need to get a confirmation of the needs of your project sponsor before submitting the draft project plan, you may want to start in People style to check understanding before moving to Process style to present your plan. If you find that your assumptions were incorrect when listening to the project sponsor, you can disengage and re-plan the project.

The outcome of this step is to identify the influence objective you need to achieve.

At the end of Step 3, you can summarise your thinking on a Planning Guide.

STEP 4: WHICH STYLE WILL GIVE THE GREATEST CHANCE OF SUCCESS?

It is probably possible to achieve your influence objective in any situation by using any one of the four styles – but some will be more appropriate and easier to use than others. This step in the planning process helps you to make that decision, and to make it based on a strategic plan, not just on personal preference and comfort.

First think about the outcome you want – a deal, solution, understanding or cooperation. As identified in Chapter 6, each style delivers a specific outcome, so the outcome you desire guides you to the ideal style to use. You can also refer to the "When to use" checklist for each style in Figure 11-7 to help you decide if the situation is suited to the style.

ACTION	PROCESS	PEOPLE	IDEAS
A deal is acceptable	A solution is acceptable	Generating understanding is the ideal outcome	You want to build co-operation
There is little time to discuss	There is time to discuss	There is time to engage in empathetic listening	There is time to connect with the other person
You both have something to exchange that the other wants	You have good ideas	You need commitment	You need commitment
Compliance is acceptable	You have good logical reasons and factual data	There are strong feelings present	You have ideas, beliefs and values in common
You have no logical reasons to support your case	You are open to rational response and debate	You are willing to share your feelings	You can envision exciting possibilities
The other party's reasons for not agreeing are better than yours in support (which means you will lose a debate in Process style)			

Figure 11-7: When to use each style

Next, consider the strength of preference of the other party – what is the "language" they respond to. It may be that you can achieve your influence goal with a tactical shift into their language. If not, you will probably need to adapt your "language" in the style you choose so that they will hear you better. It may also be that their strength of preference is such that you need to go back to Step 3 and define a sequence with a new influence objective to help you plan the sequence steps.

Finally, you can reflect on what would be the impact of each of the styles. It is not the intention that you use all of the styles, but just thinking through the scenario of what would happen if you used Action, Process, People or Ideas. This will give you an insight into which will give you the best opportunity of success.

This thinking will help you to make a strategic decision about which approach will have the greatest chance of success. The answer should be emerging; possibly there are a couple of strong alternatives. If so, you can check these out in a dress rehearsal (see Step 5).

Summarise your thinking on the Planning Guide.

STEP 5: HOW DO I DO IT?

Having chosen the probable style(s) that will give the best chance of success, think about how you are going to do it.

What are the two actions from the style in the context of this situation? Can you write a storyboard[28] of the interaction? What about the words, music and dance?

---

[28] Developing a series of scenes that the discussion will progress through, like the scenes in a movie. This is not the full script, but a visualisation of the sequence of exchanges and events, including the physical environment.

What about the physical environment – how might you need to organise the interaction?

Do some risk assessment and contingency planning. Where might the difficulties occur? How will you respond to them? Do you have a plan to disengage effectively (break off the discussion so you can go back to re-planning, if only for a few seconds), if you are not getting what you want?

Returning to Mark's and Anne-Marie's case studies, the further steps can now be completed:

CASE STUDY: MARK'S PROJECT

Mark's priorities from Step 1 were:

- Influence Kim, his deputy to take on more responsibility in the short-term;
- Build a better relationship with the Research Manager;
- Strengthen the relationship with the R&D Director; and
- Understand the specific stakeholder interests for this project so that he could focus his thinking in the right direction.

He constructed a series of individual plans based on the preferences of the individuals and the outcome needed. With Kim, there was a very close relationship and no need for relationship building. He could take a very direct approach, use Action style to clarify what he wanted her to do, and what she could expect in return. This would be relatively easy, as Action was Mark's preferred style and Kim liked it too.

When it came to the next priorities, Mark would have more difficulty. In order to build relationships and understand needs, Mark could see that he would have to use People style a lot, possibly with some Ideas style to strengthen relationships. People style was his least

---

149

preferred style, so he would need a lot of practice and preparation in order to be comfortable. He would have to slow down and focus more on the relationship rather than the task. But it was clear from the planning that that was the style that would get the desired result. He could not build a relationship with the Research Manager by using his preferred Action style!

CASE STUDY: ANNE-MARIE'S KEY ACCOUNT PLANNING

Anne-Marie's first priority was to build a better relationship with Andrea, the Technical Manager at the customer. She needed to check her assumptions about Andrea's position as an adversary and build trust. It would be good to think that it was possible to turn Andrea into an Ally, but if not, then Anne-Marie needed to know what objections there were, so that she could then put together detailed arguments (Process) or construct a deal (Action) that could give her a chance of success.

So following through the next planning steps with respect to Andrea, Anne-Marie planned a meeting to start to build a relationship, probably needing to use People style to share perceptions and to seek to understand where Andrea was positioning herself. Depending on the outcome of this first influence objective – understanding Andrea's position – Anne-Marie could then move on to use Ideas style to present a positive image of working together, or disengage to plan how to deal with Andrea's confirmed opposition. Anne-Marie was comfortable with People and Ideas style, so just needed to work out how to open the conversation with Andrea.

Next, Anne-Marie and her team considered the two Fence-Sitters and followed through their planning. When it came to Bill, the General Manager and Lucas, the

Production Lead, no-one in Anne-Marie's team knew them or had a possibility to make a direct contact. So they decided to use their internal Allies to help determine where they were placed in terms of the contract and the relationship with their company.

Peter, as Engineering Lead worked closely with production, so Anne-Marie would influence him to sound Lucas out. The impact on production was further down the project timeline, so it was not imperative to build a direct relationship immediately; what they don't want is a "loose cannon" at the early stages. Peter had a very strong preference for Process style, so a logical, structured argument would work best with him. Anne-Marie was open to other possibilities of getting Lucas off the fence, so Process would work well. Unfortunately, it was not her preferred style, so she knew that she would need to practice how to approach Peter in order to feel comfortable.

With Bill, the General Manager, it was more important to find a way of building an immediate and direct relationship. He was in a much stronger position to influence this contract, and future decisions. It was worth putting in the effort to try to build a strong, long-term relationship with him. So Anne-Marie would influence Peter and Geert to get her an introduction to Bill, so that she could meet him and start the process of relationship building. Again, Process style would seem to be the best option for influencing Peter and Geert, but then Anne-Marie would be more into her comfort zone of People and Ideas when meeting with Bill to build the relationship.

In the case studies, both Mark and Anne-Marie made choices on what style to use based on what would give them the best chance of achieving the outcome that they wanted, not based on their degree of comfort with the style itself. Sometimes the outcome of the planning is to confirm your preferred choice – like with Mark and Kim. In other situations, the planning process will lead you to using a style that you are less comfortable and confident in using. So, from the 5-step planning process comes a further action step: Practice.

You need to rehearse your plan to become confident, refine it, check out any alternatives and prepare for different responses:

- Find someone to work with who can take the role of the other party in your scenario. Give them a short (2 minute maximum) brief on how the person usually responds.

- Now try out the plan you developed for this scenario. You play yourself, the other person plays the role of your target. Spend your time rehearsing with the other person in the way that you have planned, not discussing the plan. You get more insight by doing, not theorising.

- Get feedback from your partner on what works, and what could be improved. Work together to develop a refined plan. If you can get another colleague to join in to work as an observer, so much the better. An observer can give more objective and focused feedback.

You should now have a plan with the best chance of success and the confidence to deliver it. If you have any doubts, go back and re-plan or re-rehearse until you are confident. Or change your influence objective – you may be trying to achieve too much. Use the "elephant eating" formula – break the problem down into bite-sized chunks.

DEVELOPMENT EXERCISES

1. WHO IS WHO?

- Identify the key relationships you have with partners, colleagues, managers, suppliers, customers, etc. Can you identify their style preference? Can you think of ways that you can adjust your "language" to better communicate with them.

- Take a real life situation and draw a Stakeholder Map of the key stakeholders. What does this map tell you about your influence priorities?

- From a different perspective, draw a Stakeholder Map of your job. What does that tell you about your strategy to be an effective contributor? Are there any major gaps? Any important relationships that are not good?

- Try completing a Stakeholder Analysis on the key stakeholders in a project you are leading, or on the stakeholders in the successful outcome of your job role? Who is working with you? Where are the Adversaries and Accomplices? What strategy do you need to pursue to improve the potential outcome for your job?

2. PLANNING

- Complete a Planning Guide for a number of different real life situations, and share your thinking with colleagues and friends to challenge your analysis.

3. REHEARSAL

- Take some of the real life plans you have made and rehearse these with some colleagues or friends.

PLANNING FOR SUCCESS

CHAPTER TWELVE

GETTING RESULTS IN MORE DIFFICULT SITUATIONS

"Everything that irritates us about others can lead us to an understanding of ourselves."
CARL JUNG

"It was impossible to get a conversation going; everybody was talking too much."
YOGI BERRA

There are some situations where simple positive influence will not work, where the situation is complex, the relationship is so bad that trust and credibility are in question, or positions have become entrenched. In these situations, you can still get results without having to refer to higher authority for arbitration or decision, but the process for reaching agreement reflects the complexity of the situation. You need to plan more carefully and engage in conflict resolution techniques to get a positive outcome.

This chapter will investigate the causes of conflict and typical resolution strategies people use, and outline an approach to negotiation that uses the four styles in a coordinated fashion to achieve a win:win result. The chapter concludes by investigating the problems faced by

155

the increasing amount of remote, cross cultural and cross functional working.

CAUSES OF CONFLICT

CASE STUDY: A CROSS CULTURAL MISUNDERSTANDING

Two car manufacturers were discussing collaboration and even a possible merger. One manufacturer was Swedish, the other French. At the initial meetings between the company boards, the Swedish team used well-constructed presentations which everyone was expected to listen to, raising any discussion points at the end of the presentation. The French company's style was to address a question or a discussion point when it arises. So there were frequent interruptions from the French managers, which were considered "rude" by the Swedish team and disrespectful to the speaker.

When it was time for the French company lead speaker to take the stand, he made a brief statement to the meeting which, in their culture, would have stimulated the rest of the board meeting to debate and have a discussion. Instead, he was greeted with silence, as the Swedish team were waiting for the detail of the presentation. They felt affronted that the French team had not put any perceived thought or effort into preparing their position, and were unable to discuss and debate without any preparation themselves.

The conclusion from these initial discussions was that each company decided it could not work with the other because of the cultural differences; despite the fact that they both needed a working partner to inject ideas, develop new models and share production costs in the increasingly competitive market.

Differences in culture – and resulting conflict – can come from a number of different sources, not just nationality or company. Earlier in the book the different cultures of Baby Boomer, Generation X and Generation Y were identified. Different professions, genders, functions, organisations, races exhibit fundamental differences in the way in which they typically behave, which can cause the same misunderstandings as between the Swedish and French car manufacturers. And different cultures are just one potential source of conflict.

Sources of conflict can be traced to an objective cause: organisation structures such as the matrix show up conflicts between the axes of the matrix; company policies and directives; the competition for limited resources; different decision-making processes; unclear objectives; differences between manager and individual expectations; and different processes and systems. Or the causes might be traced to a more psychological root: differences in personal values and beliefs; cultural background; behaviour; lack of clarity of role; difficult relationships; and personal sensitivity.

Whatever the cause, the outcome can be traumatic, negative and unproductive. People often expend more energy fighting battles inside organisations than they do fighting the competition outside. To make matters worse, many of the strategies that are deployed to deal with these conflicts merely control the conflict and may legitimise and prolong it. So, regulatory responses such as arbitration or the imposition of new rules and procedures do not deal with the underlying issues and leave the causes of the conflict in place to emerge again later. Competing, pressurising one side over the other or trying to resolve conflict through application of force does not work either, as they radically undermine the long-term relationship.

To achieve a long lasting solution to the conflict, you need to confront it in an environment where collaboration is possible and you can negotiate a mutually acceptable outcome, where both parties are happy – the so called win:win solution.

USING INQUIRY AND ADVOCACY TO ACHIEVE A SUCCESSFUL OUTCOME

If both parties are talking to each other, and one party is willing to take the initiative to find a resolution, then conflicts can be addressed using the process of Inquiry and Advocacy outlined in Chapter 5. Starting with **Inquiry**, use People style to find out about the conflict situation from the other party's perspective. How do they see the situation? Can you see it from their perspective? Pretend you don't know anything (you need to suspend your own thoughts and position on the issue), and try to learn as much as possible about their point of view.

A word of warning – you are not listening in order to catch them out or find fault with their reasoning, however tempting that is. You are not trying to win a debate, you are trying to resolve a conflict through dialogue. You need to be able to see the issue from the other person's perspective so you understand. You do not have to agree with it – it is not a capitulation or acceptance of the other's arguments as "right" or "correct", just an acknowledgment that it is their point of view, which is valid for them and that you can understand. If you feel inclined to push back, defend your position, or play "gotcha", take note, step back a pace in the inquiry, and start to listen again with the intent to understand. That may mean admitting your poor listening and inquiry skill: *"I'm sorry, I realise I've just started to develop some counter-arguments in my thinking, and I have therefore missed what you were just saying. I am really trying to understand your position, so would you mind explaining that last point to me again."* This honesty shows your desire to inquire not persuade or manipulate, and will be respected.

The outcome of a successful inquiry is to acknowledge the views of the other party – show that you've heard and understood. Try to get to a position that you can make the other party's case for them. Once again it is worth making the point that acknowledgment is not agreement. This is difficult for British or others who have been brought up in a tradition of debate and persuasion. You are saying, "This sounds really important to you" doesn't mean you are going to go along with their decision.

When you get to the point that the other party has accepted that you understand their perspective on the topic, it's your turn. Use Process style and the following tips for effective **advocacy** to put your side: present your case as an option not a final conclusion, present clearly and directly in manageable chunks, use observable / measurable data and examples to support your reasoning, clarify your position without minimising theirs. You will typically find that as you have put the effort in to understand, and you are presenting calmly and not in definitive conclusions, people will listen to you.

Now you can start to build solutions together. From a common pool of data, you can work together to build a new conclusion that is acceptable to both parties. If this becomes adversBook Antiqua at any time, go back to inquiry to understand why. The process is shown diagrammatically in Figure 12-1.

Figure 12-1: Using Inquiry and Advocacy to create a new successful outcome

GETTING WIN:WIN OUTCOMES THROUGH NEGOTIATION

The more the two parties are separated by conflicting interests, the more they need to revert to negotiation in order to achieve a successful outcome. Negotiation is an advanced form of influence, where instead of just planning a strategy to get what you want whilst maintaining or building the relationship, you need to put as much effort (if not more) into making sure that the other party gets what they want as well. The successful outcome is determined when both parties are equally happy – a win:win outcome.

This view of negotiation differs from some tactical variants of the use of the term, where one party uses various tactics in order to gain an extra advantage over the other – in effect operating a win:lose strategy. This by its nature can only work in one-off situations, as in most cases the "loser" will know they have come off worst and will take the next opportunity to get their own back. So win:lose inevitably becomes lose:lose in the long term.

To be able to succeed at win:win negotiation, you must first adopt a mindset of collaboration – you will stand up for your position and needs but simultaneously respect and cooperate with the other party's position and needs. This allows you to deal with the conflict between the two sets of needs and work to a solution, without avoiding the conflict altogether or weighing one set of needs over the other in an overly competitive or accommodating mindset. Any of these latter strategies may well deal with the conflict but will not resolve it in a satisfactory way.[29]

Compromise is the trap that many conflict resolution strategies tend to fall into. The expectation that there will need to be some give and take in order to find a solution means that people too readily seek some expedient solution that only partially satisfies the parties. It falls halfway between competing and accommodating. Splitting the difference or seeking a quick middle-ground solution usually leaves both parties feeling that they are equally unhappy, with their needs not acknowledged and the real source of the conflict not addressed. Collaboration may take longer and be more difficult, but it is worthwhile for long-term relationship building and for finding permanent solutions to conflicts.

---

[29] These mindsets are explained and developed in the Thomas-Kilmann Conflict Mode Instrument -- also known as the TKI published by CPP, Inc, Menlo Park, CA.

THE OPEC APPROACH TO WIN:WIN NEGOTIATIONS

As negotiation is a process, there are a number of phases that need to be successfully completed to achieve an outcome. The OPEC model (see figure 12-2) describes these phases:

OPENING   POSITIONING   EXPLORING   CLOSING

Figure 12-2: The OPEC model

Each phase of the OPEC model: Opening, Positioning, Exploring and Closing has a number of actions that need to be completed and an outcome to achieve before moving to the next phase.

In the Opening phase, the purpose is to create a positive climate with the intended outcome that the two parties can continue to cooperate and collaborate in the rest of the negotiation. The focus is on building the relationship, establishing the common ground and agreeing the ground rules for the continuation of the negotiation.

In the Positioning phase, the focus is on stating – and testing – each other's position on the issue, initially to see whether there is an easy solution that can be derived from logical problem-solving with the data and reasoning to hand, or whether the gap between the two parties' positions is such that there is a need to move further in the negotiation process. There is no way that one party can influence or persuade the other at this point.

Moving then to **Exploring**, you probe and identify the other party's underlying needs for the negotiation; to understand what they really want. As you probe and understand what is driving their position, then you can usually find alternative ways of satisfying these needs which were not immediately obvious to either party in the positioning phase. As you also disclose my own underlying needs, more possibilities emerge which allow for possible exchanges to be tested to see whether they meet the underlying needs of the two parties.

Exploring is the crucial stage of a negotiation; most discussions fail to reach agreement as one party keeps trying to persuade the other party that their ideas for a solution are the best (they are at the top of the ladder of inference, discussing conclusions). They confuse what they **want** (our position) with what they **need**.

CASE STUDY: JIM WANTS A SANDWICH

Jim wakes up in the middle of the night and wants a sandwich. He goes down to the kitchen to discover there is no bread, no butter, no cheese, and no ham. He is just about to go back to bed, unhappy that he can't get what he wants. Then, he recognises that his desire for the sandwich is just a want, and his underlying need is to satisfy hunger; he notices some alternatives in the kitchen, like some fruit from the fruit bowl, takes a banana and goes back to bed happy that his need is satisfied.

You will only find the possible alternatives if you understand that your want (position) is just one way of satisfying your underlying need – the solution you came up with first, but by no means the only possible solution. Understanding your needs and the other party's needs are critical to finding win:win outcomes.

Once you have explored the options and possibilities uncovered in the Exploring phase, it is possible to finally put together a deal in the Closing stage, assemble the package and make an agreement that now satisfies both parties.

If you look at the actions and desired outcome for each phase, then a pattern also emerges regarding which of the four influence styles will be most effective in each phase. In the Opening phase you want to ensure cooperation with the other party, so the predominant style should be Ideas: you need to highlight the common ground and connection that exists and envision a successful and positive outcome to the negotiation in order to create a positive and forward-looking climate.

In the Positioning phase, the focus is on bringing in your data and analysis and making a statement about your own position, or potential solution to the problem. You engage in debate and discussion with the other party, weighing up the options. The predominant style is Process.

Moving to Exploring, the need is to probe and listen to the discover and understand the underlying needs and wants of the other party, and to share your own thinking about your needs in order to open up new possibilities and options for exchange. The best style here is People.

Finally, when you put together the deal in the Closing stage, the style will be Action: the demand and exchange from both sides is the final agreement.

So, in a negotiation, each one of the four styles is used in a sequence in order to get the desired result as shown in Figure 12-3:

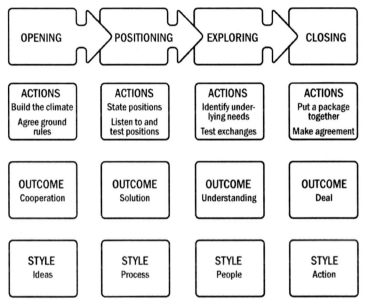

Figure 12-3: The actions, outcomes and dominant style for each phase of the OPEC process

CASE STUDY: RESOLVING AN INTERDEPARTMENTAL DISPUTE

The Omega Corporation works in the electronics industry, specialising in the application of new technology to industrial measurement. It has four main departments, Technology, Application, Manufacturing and Sales, with a small administrative and support centre.

The Technology Department is responsible for identifying new technologies for measurement, either from its own laboratories or through joint projects and liaison with university technology departments around the world.

The Application Department takes over the new technologies and ensures that they are commercially viable before putting together a business plan for their manufacture and promotion.

The Manufacturing Department is responsible for in-house and contract manufacture of the hardware and software of existing and new technologies. The Sales Department is the liaison between the customer and the company. Many of the ideas for potential new technologies come from Sales who have identified a customer need.

The relationship between the departments is usually good, though they do work to different goals and performance measures. The Technology Department prides itself on its innovation, and its good working relationships with the University technology research departments from where a lot of the cutting–edge ideas originate. Some of the ideas are technically great, but are not economically viable, which is a fact of life. But the Technology Department often feel that the Application Department is too cautious in their analysis and delay getting new products into the marketplace with the outcome that the potential to lead the industry in technology is lost.

Commercial viability is the basis of the reputation for the Application Department. They pride themselves on making sure that there is always value added to the company and that there are no expensive mistakes caused through lack of proper testing or evaluation of the technology. Too often, the Technology Department delivers urgent projects to you, often with little testing. There seems to be little awareness of the commercial aspects of the business.

Pat, the Application Department Manager is about to meet with Johan, the Technology Department Manager about a new measurement device for the drinks industry that will significantly reduce the wastage in the blending of ingredients. The idea came from one of the sales engineers who had observed difficulties in creating the right mix at a customer premises last year, and this new technology has been developed in a joint project with a University.

Johan wants a quick acceptance by Application and to get the product into the market before the competitors. Pat is more cautious and wants to make sure it is a viable product, and already has a number of other trials of technologies under way. The University came up with a quick result, and the initial technical review is excellent. Johan and Pat are set for conflict.

Opening phase: Pat and Johan agreed to meet in a meeting room at the office rather than one of their own offices. This helped to set the climate as they were on "neutral ground"; neither was risking being perceived as using position power. The atmosphere was friendly – they did have a generally good relationship – and they spent time reflecting on the common ground and successful discussions they had in the past. They agreed that it was most likely that this discussion would be equally positive and they could both see a successful outcome *(Ideas style)*. The timetable for the discussion was agreed and that a verbal form of agreement was all that was required. When both parties felt comfortable that they were ready to proceed, they moved into the Positioning phase – making sure that they spent enough time in the Opening phase and not rushing to get to Positioning without the relationship necessary for success.

Positioning phase: As Johan was the party with the most urgency, he stated his position first. They had a customer need, a new technology had been devised which worked well in initial trials. There were three competitors known to be working in the same area, so getting the system into production and into the market as soon as possible would be essential for the company. He wanted to fast track the Application process. A proposal for achieving this would be to put a development version into the customer premises and do some of the testing on site so that they could get the publicity. He was willing to help out with supplying some engineer resource to the test as he knew that the Application Department were already stretched in testing and developing business cases for other products. *(Process style)*

Pat asked a few questions to check her understanding of the situation and the technology, then stated her position. Whilst she recognised that the initial results looked promising, and there was a clear commercial opportunity in the industry, she must ensure that the project has viability before going public. She had to guard against the bad publicity that could come from announcing a breakthrough too early if it did not work in practice. The costs of putting a failure right, far outweighed the opportunities for an early advantage. As she had only heard of this new technology in the last month, it had not been possible to plan the evaluation trials into their schedule. There was insufficient funding to cover the costs of all products, so priorities must be set. In this case Pat estimated that testing would take about two months to complete, and it would be at least two more months before the current workload and the holiday season allowed a start. *(Process style)*

Johan challenged some of Pat's arguments and reminded her that he had foreseen the staffing difficulty and had offered to second some of his engineers to Applications to help with the testing. Pat would not have to bear the burden of cost, just oversee the process. However, Pat countered again that even with this offer to deal with the cost issue; there was still a fundamental difficulty with releasing a product to the market that had not been properly evaluated, and all of the risks that were associated. They were beginning to reach an impasse. Despite amassing all of the arguments they could to persuade the other, little movement was taking place towards an agreement that satisfied both. Fearing that they would get stuck, Pat decided to move away from Positioning.

Exploring phase: Pat recognised that Johan was fiercely defending his position and was trying to find every possible way to get this product into the market early. It was an interesting product, and it had some real potential in that there was at least one ready-made customer, but why is this product so important? *"Johan, you seem particularly energised by this particular product and want to get it into the market quickly. I think I understand the commercial and technology leading future that you foresee for this product, but you don't always support cases with such vigour. So am interested in why this product, and why now? What is driving this for you Johan?" (People style)*

Recognising that Pat seemed really interested to understand, Johan disclosed that he was under pressure from the Managing Director to cut costs – nothing unusual there but this time the MD was looking to reduce the university project funding. The MD saw this area having few controls, little direction and poor performance in identifying commercial products.

Pat confirmed her understanding – here was a potentially great commercial product that had been developed by one of the University partnerships, and if this went into the market quickly, Johan would have some data to counter the MD's push to cut the funding in this area. *"If that is the real need driving your desire to get this product fast-tracked, are you open to other suggestions that would keep the University funding that did not mean taking a risk on this product?"* Johan said he would be but could not see any other way. He was also interested to find out why Pat had been so adamant that even though he was offering to cover the cost of the Application testing himself, she was still not willing to move her position. What was driving her reluctance? *(People style)*

Pat disclosed that she and her department had been subject to a few criticisms from the Board in recent months over the poor returns on some products that were not in line with the business cases. She had identified that most of these products were rushed into the market for one reason or another, and her department had not had enough time to consider them properly. She could not afford to take another risk regarding a product launch – her own credibility and career was at stake. She needed more time to consider developments in a calm atmosphere, not be pressurised into making a rushed decision.

Johan could now see why Pat was reluctant to release this product, and that his own behaviour in not involving Pat at early stages of design could cause her to feel more under pressure in making decisions. He could see that if he brought Pat into discussions much earlier, it could help to protect her from what she saw as a great personal risk. He could build a number of Pat's concerns into the design at the initial stages.

It looked as though there was a potential for agreement that met each of their needs.

Closing phase: Pat and Johan exchanged their offers, to put together a deal. Johan recognised Pat's need to be seen to be credible and competent in fulfilling the success criteria for her department in the eyes of the Board. He offered to bring her in on new projects at the initial stages in the future and build a close liaison with the Application Department to take early account of concerns in the design, and to give Pat more time and information for evaluation.

In return, Pat recognised that Johan was under extreme pressure from the MD, and offered to have a meeting with the Board to support the case for continued University funding, putting together an analysis of recent commercial successes that came from that route which would prove that they more than covered the cost. She was confident the Board and the MD would agree when they saw the numbers. They had a deal, without the need to fast-track the current technology proposal. *(Action style)*

REMOTE WORKING

Trying to get results when you don't have the authority is difficult, and when the person you are trying to influence is not in the same location, the difficulties increase. You have to make more contact by telephone or e-mail. These media are generally far less satisfying from a human standpoint than doing something face to face. You are deprived of the opportunity to observe the expressions and body language of the people with whom you are communicating, from which you pick up a massive amount of information, as discussed in Chapter 5.

At least on the telephone you can hear if someone is hesitating, you can pay attention to the tone of their voice. Even so, some observers on remote team working have suggested that you needed to spend up to five times longer in the social conversation or on the telephone to have the same impact in building relationships in face to face teams. As people typically do not spend even the same amount of time – "OK, everyone is online, let's get down to business, this call is costing money..." – it is easy to see how misunderstandings and conflicts can easily arise. When it comes down to written communication, it is far easier to generate misunderstanding, hence the use of "smileys" in e-mails.

The determined and frequent use of People style will help to minimise misunderstandings: continually checking understanding, slowing down the communication to make sure everyone is moving at the same pace, seeking to understand the cause of any differences, giving others who may be less comfortable with the situation the opportunity to express themselves.

Using People style can also help the remote manager to understand each team members' individual needs and adapt to them.

CASE STUDY: ELAINE'S REMOTE TEAM

Elaine, took over a project that had a number of contributors who were working from home or remote bases. She continued the previous manager's practice of calling each of the team members individually each day, and having a team conference call each week. After a few weeks of this regime, she became aware that Jim, one of her team, seemed to be unhappy with the daily phone call – after probing and listening to him, she discovered that Jim felt that he was being checked up on and that Elaine did not trust him.

Elaine took this feedback and, fearing this might be the impression she was giving to others as well, stopped calling the team members routinely every day, waiting until the weekly conference call to catch up and only calling at other times when there was something specific to discuss.

This seemed to work well, then Elaine sensed that another team member, Sophie, was not happy. On listening to her reasons, Elaine discovered that Sophie liked the daily contact and when it stopped she was left feeling that Elaine did not care about her and that she was not being appreciated. Sophie found working from home to be very isolating and lonely and needed more support and reassurance.

So, Elaine concluded that she had to set up a personal regime for each team member based on his or her own needs – she would need to spend some time listening to each one in order to discover what was important to them.

There is at least one advantage to telephone influencing or negotiating – you can have your notes and plans in front of you, and they do not detract from your presence as they might in a face-to-face meeting. To be even more influential, as the focus of attention is entirely on the voice, you can exaggerate the voice tone to get your message emphasis understood. One easy way to do this is to exaggerate the dance of the style – if you want to sound assertive, stand up; if you want to sound pleased, smile; if you want to listen, lean forward and take up an open position. And listen actively and empathetically.

With all forms of modern communication, there is a sense of immediacy and the need for instant responses. So be aware that you might be tempted into making fast, unwise decisions. There is nothing wrong in saying to the other party something like, *"What you have been saying has given me several things to think about, I need a few moments to consider what you've said,"* or *"Let me give that idea some serious consideration – I will call you back in 10 minutes."* That gives you time to consider what is being said in a calm, reflective way and gives you time to plan to make the appropriate response. But don't forget to return the call or email at the time you promised, or you lose trust and credibility in the eyes of the other party.

CROSS CULTURAL/CROSS FUNCTIONAL WORKING

When you are preparing for a conversation with people from another culture (and other functions or departments are really just examples of other cultures), you should do some careful research, even before you start any actual planning, especially if it is a new culture to you. The danger is always that you may end up re-enacting the French / Swedish story at the start of the chapter.

Read all you can find on the culture involved, to make yourself aware of the social norms and expectations so that you are not inadvertently rude. Most of these social norms – like not showing the soles of your feet in an Arab country – are universal. But not all of the cultural norms and rules which most culture books contain apply to everyone. Most culture books and checklists are generalisations, and not everyone complies with the stereotypes, especially with the increasing internationalisation of our behaviour that is brought about by travel and the media. But until you build an understanding and a relationship it is worth erring on the side of caution. For instance, do not assume that the German manager you are calling is happy with an informal salutation – start with Herr Schmidt, or Herr Doctor Schmidt as appropriate and wait to be invited to call him Hans.

Other cultural issues may emerge. For instance in individualistic cultures (Northern Europe, North America) commonly the message itself is all there needs to be for the receiver to respond or take action. A one line email request is enough. However, if the receiver is from a more collective culture (in varying degrees - Southern, Eastern Europe, Asia, Latin America) they need to know the context of the message in order to respond:

- Who (status, role) is the sender?
- Why was this message written?
- Who else in my organisation knows about this or needs to know about it?
- What consensus or permission do I need from others in order to respond?[30]

---

[30] These cultural tips are taken from *Culture matters: A barrier analysis of 30 cultural factors affecting distributed workplaces* by Dr. George F. Simons, and

Some people are very informal in emails. This can come across as rude, angry or impersonal. Email is useful when you want a quick response, but if the question is not framed correctly it can damage the relationship. Similarly, more collective cultures often favour personal face-to-face meetings, videoconferencing and telephone conversations over discussion forums, instant messaging and e-mail. In some cultures surfacing conflict publicly is deemed immature while others see a good argument as bringing the best out of people.

All of these hurdles are set like traps to catch out even the best intentioned, so if there are distance and cultural issues involved, then planning and doing your homework really pays off. Adopting a People style approach, recognising that your way is not the only way and really trying to understand the important things for the other culture and individuals is the quickest way to achieve cultural flexibility. This will be appreciated more than the stereotypical Englishman who speaks slower and louder in English and expects the other party to change.

DEVELOPMENT EXERCISES

1. CONFLICT

- Identify the difficult situations and conversations you have. What are the sources of conflict here? What strategies do you typically use to resolve these difficult situations? How successful are you? Can you identify how you could get a better outcome?

---

published by George Simons International. For more cross cultural advice and information go to www.georgesimons.com and www.diversophy.com, tel +1 (831) 531-4706 or +33 4 92 97 57 35

2. USING INQUIRY AND ADVOCACY

- The next time you find yourself "triggered" into a defensive reaction by something the other person has said or done, instead of responding in your automatic way, become curious and inquire into what it was that caused your response. Take time to inquire and fully understand the other person before stating your opinion.

- If you have a real disagreement with someone, and it is important for you to have a good working relationship, practise inquiry and advocacy to see if you can identify a common set of data on which you can jointly form some analysis to come up with a new conclusion or solution, using the process described in Figure 12-1.

3. NEGOTIATION

- The next time you need to negotiate something, take some time out to plan your approach using the OPEC model, and think about each of the action steps and styles to use in each phase:

  o Those who are stronger in the emotive styles of People and Ideas will need to plan to put their Positioning case clearly and logically using Process style, and recognise the need to move to a close using Action style and not stay too long in the Exploring phase.

  o Those who are stronger in the task oriented styles of Process and Action will need to spend longer thinking about and planning Opening and Exploring. They will tend not to spend enough time in either phase. They will be uncomfortable in Opening and move on to the task before the other party may be ready. They will also spend too long trying to persuade the other party of their solution, or solutions, in the Positioning phase, and not switch to People in order to identify underlying needs.

4. REMOTE AND CROSS CULTURAL WORKING

- Reflect on the different cultures that you work with. What do you know about them? What differences can you identify? Read up as much as you can on them and check out your assumptions with the people you know in the cultures – taking note of any differences you find.

- Get some feedback on how you come across – ask your friends from other cultures or functions how you (and your culture / function) are perceived. How do you come across? What unintended cultural traps are you falling into? How would they like you to behave?

- Whenever you travel to a different country or visit a different organisation, pay attention to how people behave. What norms and rituals do you see? How do people respond to each other? Check your observations and assumptions with a member of that country or organisation.

- Check with your colleagues how they like working in remote and virtual teams. What do they need in order to be effective? How do they want you to respond to them? What technologies work best for them in terms of communication?

CHAPTER THIRTEEN

MOVING ON – OPTIONS FOR FURTHER DEVELOPMENT

"If people knew how hard I worked to get my mastery, it wouldn't seem so wonderful after all."
MICHELANGELO

"The more I practice, the luckier I get."
GARY PLAYER

Each of the chapters contained some development exercises to help you build the awareness, understanding and skills associated with that section. But you will have realised by now, that just this limited amount of practice in developing new skills and approaches will not be sufficient to give you the confidence to do something different in the workplace – especially taking the risk of using a very underused style in a critical situation with one of your key partners. This book has been one step on your learning journey to getting results without authority, but by no means the last. This final chapter therefore gives some suggestions for further development – things you can do on your own, like reading or individual practice; and things you can do with others, like attending a training course or working with other like minded colleagues in a learning support group.

WWW.GETTINGRESULTSWITHOUTAUTHORITY.COM

There is a dedicated website for *Getting Results without Authority*, with a regular blog and resources such as tips and techniques. You can download copies of the Planning Guide for use in your real life situations, and read further into the whole subject of being successful in modern organisations. There are links to related subject areas such as positive political skills, negotiation and performance management. You can contribute questions, join in discussions, share your success stories and link to other learners in the art of positive influence. This is an opportunity for you to join the learning community and get further support and challenges to continue your development.

CONTINUING DEVELOPMENT

Developing behavioural skill is not something that can be done from reading a book alone. You need to practise the behaviours in order to become proficient to develop the confidence in making some changes and also to get feedback on the impact of your intended change. You cannot do this on your own.

One of the best ways to develop your skill further is to attend a training course where you can learn with other participants from similar and different backgrounds, who all have the same goal of improving their ability to influence positively. The first course to recommend is the "course of the book": *Getting Results Without Authority*, run regularly as a 2 day public access course by Frost & Sullivan in London and Brussels. (www.frost.com).

Another course which addresses the subject and whose roots are in the same original research, but does so from a more personal development standpoint is Focus on Influence run by Learning Consortium (www.learningconsortium.eu). Learning Consortium run a limited number of public access programmes each year of 3.5 days duration, in both English and Dutch.

You can form a learning support group with friends and colleagues, and use the development exercises in the book for inspiration to learn together and challenge each other to develop. Bringing real life situations to this group, discussing a potential plan and then rehearsing the plan (and alternatives), with someone taking the role of the other party, is the closest you can get to reality. It is therefore a great learning experience, without the added risk of trying out your plan without testing it first.

Other situations lend themselves to practice: places where you are never likely to return are low risk situations, and can be places where you can afford to take some more risk yourself and try something out which you wouldn't want to do, for instance, with your boss until you had developed more confidence. Hotels, shops and restaurants when you are on holiday are great places to try out your negotiation and influence skills, as long as it is not a regular location for you! It doesn't matter too much if you make a mistake, get it wrong, or make a mess of the relationship. Once you think about it, there are a myriad of opportunities for you to practise.

READING LIST

Although reading a book will not change your behaviour, they can give you insight and tips. There are a massive amount of books written on the subject of influence and communication skills. A search of titles including "influence" on Amazon brought up over 43,000 results! So I have selected a few that have influenced my thinking and that I would recommend. Many are quoted in the text:

FIRSTLY SOME GENERALLY GOOD BOOKS ON INFLUENCE AND INTERPERSONAL SKILLS:

The 7 Habits of Highly Effective People by Stephen R. Covey (Simon & Schuster, ISBN 0-671-66398-4) deals with seven principles that underpin personal effectiveness and communication that mirror a number of the principles of this book: begin with the end in mind, think win/win and seek first to understand then to be understood.

The Empowered Manager by Peter Block (Jossey-Bass, ISBN 1-55542-019-2) is the source of the stakeholder matrix used in Chapter 11, and is also a practical guide to using positive political skills at work. For readers involved in internal or external consulting, Peter's book *Flawless Consulting* (University Associates, ISBN 0-89384-052-1) is invaluable.

Two books by Judith E. Glaser *Creating We* (Platinum Press, ISBN 1-59337-268-X) and *The DNA Of Leadership* (Platinum Press, ISBN 1-59337-518-2) have one major theme – leading organisations to be more caring, moving thinking from being I-centred to being WE-centred and away from blame cultures and groupthink.

Bill Noonan has written an extremely readable book intended to help individuals avoid getting caught up in a cycle of "defensive routines" highlighted in Chapter 5, which comes with its own DVD case study to help develop your skills: *Discussing the Undiscussable: A Guide to Overcoming Defensive Routines in the Workplace* by William R. Noonan, (Jossey-Bass. ISBN 978-0-7879-8632).

Finally, *Influence – The Psychology of Persuasion* by Robert B. Cialdini (HarperCollins, ISBN 978-0-06-124189-5) is a classic bestseller on why people say "yes."

ON INFLUENCING ACROSS CULTURES:

There are any number of books on etiquette and cultural manners appropriate to different countries, which are a ready source of information on the basic "do's" and "don'ts" for any traveller to a new culture. These are easily available at airport bookshops, and it is always worth reading up on your own culture so that you are more aware of your own culture and impact on others. For British readers, I can recommend two: The classic *How to be a Brit* by George Mikes (Penguin, ISBN 0 14 008179 8) and the more recent *Watching the English: The Hidden Rules of English Behaviour* by Kate Fox (Hodder & Stoughton, ISBN 0 34 081886 7).

For more in depth understanding of the dimensions of culture in nations and corporations, and how to use these in a positive way, two books are "must-haves": *Cultures and Organisation - Software of the Mind: Intercultural Cooperation and its Importance for Survival* by Geert Hofstede (McGraw-Hill, ISBN 0 07 029307 4) and *Riding the Waves of Culture: Understanding diversity in global business* by Fons Trompenaars. (McGraw-Hill, ISBN 0 7863 1125 8).

Anyone (male or female) who does not understand the differences between male and female communication needs to read this book: *Talking from 9 to 5 - Women and men at work: Language, sex and power* by Deborah Tannen (Virago, ISBN 1 86049 200 2) which deals with the conversational style of men and women in the workplace, and how the differences can lead to major misunderstanding. Deborah Tannen is also the author of the best-selling title: *You Just Don't Understand*, which also deals with cross gender communication.

Why Men Don't Listen & Women Can't Read Maps by Allan and Barbara Pease (Pease International, ISBN 0-957-81081-4) and *Men are from Mars, Women are from Venus* by John

Gray (Thorsons, ISBN 0-7225-2840-X) deal with the subject of cross-gender communication more light heartedly, but with no less substance.

ON NEGOTIATION:

Two books stand out in the area of win/win negotiation. They were two of the first books on the subject, and are yet to be surpassed: *Getting to yes: negotiating agreement without giving in* by Roger Fisher and William Ury (Arrow Books, ISBN 0-395-31757-6) was the initial text of the outcome of the Harvard Negotiation Project research on principled negotiation. The second, written by one of the collaborators is equally readable, enlightening and practical: *Getting Past No: Negotiating your way from confrontation to cooperation* by William Ury (Bantam Books, ISBN: 0-533-37131-2).

Finally, a couple of other classics: *Nonviolent Communication: A Language of Compassion*, by Marshall B. Rosenberg (PuddleDancer Press, ISBN: 1-892005-02-6) emphasises identifying and expressing feelings, listening empathically and direct and honest communication in a way that gets results while building relationships, which is at the heart of this book. *The collected papers of Roger Harrison*, by Roger Harrison (McGraw-Hill, ISBN 0-07-709090-X) is a collection of one of my mentors' ground-breaking papers on role negotiation, organisation culture, power and influence, and many other subjects which have formed the foundations and signposts of my journey.

GLOSSARY OF TERMS

Although many of the terms in use in this book may be familiar to readers, some may not be as well known, so a glossary of some of the management concepts and terms used in the book are included for reference[31]:

Action style	A style of communicating where people are task-oriented, keen to get things done, decisive and direct. They bargain with people to get a deal. (cf. Ideas, Process and People styles)
Advocacy	Expressing your position in clear, reasoned statements that explain the data selected as important, the meaning attached and the conclusions drawn. (cf. Inquiry)
Baby Boomers	People born between the end of World War II (1946) to about 1964. This post war generation tend to have a competitive nature and a willingness and ability to sustain hard work. Their parents had experienced the hardships of war and the Great Depression and instilled values of loyalty, career mindedness and industriousness. Today, as they face increasing responsibilities for the care of aging parents and growing children, they are re-examining their careers and looking for ways to bring new balance to their lives, also learning from their Generation

---

[31] Acknowledgement: Many of the definitions are taken from Wikipedia.

X children. They are looking forward to more time freedom, but one that is active, with 80% planning to work at least part-time in their retirement years. (cf. Generation X and Generation Y)

Cross functional team

A group of people with different functional expertise working toward a common goal. For instance a cross functional team may include people from finance, marketing, operations, and human resources departments. It may include employees from all levels of an organisation. Cross-functional teams often function best when responding to broad, rather than specific directives, such as corporate strategy and direction. They tend to respond to consensus decision making rather than hierarchical. (cf. Matrix management)

Generation X

People born between about 1965 and 1976, Generation Xers are often dubbed the "free agents" – they went to work in a chaotic, no guarantees work world. Their Baby-Boomer parents gave them independent childhoods which led them to seek autonomy and independence in the workplace. They seek opportunities to make a visible difference and use their creative abilities. They saw Baby Boomers devoting their lives to their work and corporations, putting personal fulfilment ahead of marriages, families and balanced living, and being rewarded with layoffs and the end of "jobs for life." So they put their own skill sets first and seek the aim to be employable. They value diverse experiences and are comfortable with job "hopping." They are also seeing work-life balance as a priority. (cf. Baby Boomers and Generation Y)

Generation Y

People born between about 1977 and 1998 – the younger siblings of Generation X – are self-confident, optimistic. independent and goal-oriented. Masters of the Internet and PC. They know that they have to survive on their own initiative in a workplace where no-one will look after you. Dubbed "the confident generation" at work, they think in terms of their personal fulfilment, asking: Is the job interesting and satisfying? Is the work meaningful and important? Generation Y are loyal, committed employees as long as their organisations provide them with variety and opportunity. They are entrepreneurial, outside-the-box thinkers who relish responsibility, demand immediate feedback, and expect a sense of accomplishment hourly. They thrive on challenging work and creative expression, love freedom and flexibility, and hate micromanagement. (cf. Baby Boomers and Generation X)

Ideas style

A style of communicating where people use their responsiveness to connect with other people's values and beliefs and build exciting possibilities for the future. They inspire people to cooperate with each other. (cf. Action, Process and People styles)

Influence
(as used in this book)

Using personal power to get someone to do something, whist maintaining or building a positive working relationship.

Inquiry

Asking well crafted questions that seek to understand the other person's position by clarifying their reasoning, assumptions, values, beliefs and data. (cf. Advocacy)

GLOSSARY OF TERMS

Ladder of Inference A metaphorical tool developed by Professor Chris Argyris that helps people to understand and describe how they reach conclusions.

Left-Hand Column A technique developed by Professor Chris Argyris and Professor Donald Schön for reflecting on our thinking by writing down our recollections of conversations that did not get the intended result. Unspoken thoughts and feelings are written in the Left Hand Column against the actual words in the Right Hand Column.

Matrix management A type of organisational management in which people with similar skills are pooled for work assignments. For example, all IT specialists may be in one IT department and report to an IT Manager, but these same specialists may be assigned to one or more different projects and report to a project manager(s) while working on that project. Therefore, each specialist has reporting lines to several managers.

Matrix organisation A organisation structure that utilises matrix management, either pooling common resources to work on different projects (cf. matrix management) but also where reporting lines are drawn with respect to geography, function, products or other difference. The matrix may be stronger in one dimension than the other, usually depicted by having "dotted line" relationships versus "straight line" relationships, the straight line usually taking precedence, or they may be balanced where there is no priority.

Non-verbal communication

The process of sending and receiving wordless messages through (a) gestures, body language, posture, facial expression and eye contact; and (b) speech elements such as voice quality, emotion, pace, rhythm, intonation and stress.

People style

A style of communicating where people are responsive to others needs and use their listening and sharing skills to build team working, synergy and shared understanding. They build empathy with people to build understanding. (cf. Action, Process and Ideas styles)

Personal power

The power derived from personal characteristics, charisma, and the trust and respect others give. This power resides in the person, not in the position or role that the person carries out. It is given by the consent of those over whom it is exercised. Typically experienced positively when used: "I do it because I *want* to." (cf. Position power)

Political mapping / analysis

The process of drawing the relationships and analysing the political decision making arena in an organisation or group of people. (cf. stakeholder mapping / analysis)

Position power

The power that derives from the position that the person holds in the hierarchy of control and authority in an organisation. Often experienced negatively when used: "I do it because I *have* to." (cf. Personal power)

Process style

A style of communicating where people are task focused but not directive or forceful, relying on logical and rational argument. They debate to find a solution. (cf. Action, Ideas and People styles)

GLOSSARY OF TERMS

Project organisation   Another name for a matrix organisation structure that is defined in one dimension by a number of different projects. (cf. matrix management, matrix organisation)

Reframing   Seeing a situation in another context that lets go limiting beliefs from one view and set of assumptions, allowing new conceptions and interpretation possibilities to develop.

Remote team   A work team that is geographically dispersed and meets face-to-face infrequently or not at all. The team members may be in different locations in the same country or scattered around the world, linked through telephone and electronic communications media. (cf. Virtual team)

Stakeholder   Someone who has an interest or a stake in the outcome of a project, event or organisation.

Stakeholder mapping / analysis   A process where all the individuals or groups that are likely to be affected by a proposed action are identified and then sorted according to how much they can affect the action and how much the action can affect them. This information is analysed to assess how the interests of those stakeholders should be addressed in a plan. (cf. political mapping / analysis)

Virtual team   A group of individuals who work across time, space, and organisational boundaries with links strengthened by webs of communication technology. They typically have complementary skills and are committed to a common purpose. Members of virtual teams communicate electronically, so they may never meet face to face. Many virtual teams consist of employees both working at home and small groups in the different geographic offices. (cf. remote team)

Win:win

A form of negotiation outcome that enables each party to achieve their needs and be equally happy. The outcome is achieved through collaboration and developing creative exchanges. This is in contrast to a competitive approach to negotiations where 'winner takes all' or win:lose.

Words, Music and Dance

A shorthand description of the elements of face-to-face communication covering the literal meaning of the verbal message (Words), the tone and nonverbal messages in the voice (Music) and the nonverbal messages in the gestures and body language (Dance).

GLOSSARY OF TERMS

NEW DIRECTIONS

New Directions is an international consultancy led by Geof Cox which provides a tailored approach to organisation, management and individual development. We help develop the structures and skills which ensures organisation and individual success; doing this through a fast and cost effective analysis, design and implementation service which is clearly focused on delivering the identified goal.

New Direction's services fall into two main areas:

1. **Management development**, where we coach individuals and design and run courses and workshops in interpersonal and management skills, including *Getting Results Without Authority.*

2. **Organisation change**, where our expertise is in the use of strength based and innovative interventions, often using participation processes such as Appreciative Inquiry and Open Space.

Founder Geof Cox has over 25 years of consulting experience based on an industry line management, HR and Learning & Development background, and brings a practical approach to business and management development.

New Directions also works through global strategic partnerships to bring experience from other business sectors, language skills, and the breadth and depth of specialist expertise usually reserved to large firms. We can assemble teams for clients with exactly the right mix of experience, without the commercial pressure to utilise specific employed individuals or sell a particular approach.

New Directions: *Big company scope with small company service.*

www.newdirections.uk.com

Also Available from Bookshaker.com

*Proven Psychological
Secrets to Help You
Beat The Office Bully*

Dr. Scott's

Verbal
Self
Defense

in
The Workplace

Dr. Daniel Scott

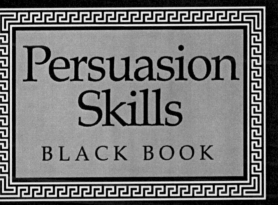

Persuasion
Skills
BLACK BOOK

Practical NLP Language Patterns for
Getting The Response You Want

Rintu Basu

FREE INSIDE
'Black Book'
Persuasion
Training
E-course

Lightning Source UK Ltd.
Milton Keynes UK
UKOW031507260612

195093UK00001B/2/P